IF YOUR LORDSHIP PLEASES

If Your Lordship Pleases

Legal Recollections

JAMES COMYN

ROUND HALL SWEET & MAXWELL

This book was typeset
by Gough Typesetting Services, Dublin for
Round Hall Sweet & Maxwell,
Brehon House,
4 Upper Ormond Quay, Dublin 7.

A catalogue record for this book
is available from the British Library.

ISBN 1-899738-45-2

By the same author

Their Friends at Court
Irish at Law
Lost Causes
Poetic Justice
Law without Gravity
Vacation Business
Wills and Intestacies (with Robert Johnson)
Summing It Up
Watching Brief
Leave to Appeal

Printed in Ireland
by Colourbooks, Dublin

If Your Lordship pleases,
And I do not think you do,
I'll repeat my arguments
and try to get them through.

'You have been accused of stealing 42,000 books. Do you swear to tell the truth, the whole truth and . . . hey! Put that back!'

Contents

1 Talk
1 The Paternity Suit
2 'Who are You?'
4 Too much Turkey
9 Doctor X
15 Do Judges remember? —
    Do Judges Regret?
20 Relegated
21 Spy Cases
23 The Surveyor
24 The Circus Gate
26 Irish Legal Studies
29 English Legal Studies
31 In Admiralty
32 Sodomy
35 An Appalling Abortion
37 Muloody's Memoirs
38 Baby Snatching
40 Frisky Phyllis
42 Cooney's Contempt
44 Complimentary
46 Concealment of Death
50 The Buck
53 Boozled
55 Indecency
56 Fired
57 Affidavit Annie
61 The King (Personally) v.
    Mylius
62 Coup de Grace
64 Unless My Eyes Deceive
    Me
65 The Song of the
    Bankrupt
65 Difference
65 Just

66 Richard Piggott
    (1829–1889)
67 When Judges make
    Mistakes
68 VAT on Legal Services
69 Doubting Thomas
71 Hard Hit Men
73 The Halsbury Handicap
    Hurdle at Haydock
74 Change
75 Clients
77 The Gold Plate
80 Roger Gray's client
80 The Coward
81 'Dear Sir – Unless'
83 Disposing of Bodies
86 Just
86 In Two Docks
87 Indecent Exposure
88 A Birmingham Riddle
89 Arson
92 Neighbours
95 The Dissenting Judgment
97 Company Fraud
99 Leonard MacNally – or
    M'Nally (1752-1820)
101 Malcolm Morris
103 Charity
104 Nurse Cadden (1956)
106 Legal Suggestions
107 Why?
108 Trust
108 Wigs, Bands and Robes
110 When Judges are wrong
110 Are Sanctions of Any
    Use?

113 An Interim Court of
     Appeal
113 Smuggling
115 Ties
117 Stories
119 Payments into Court
119 A Jury
122 Forfeiture
123 Question Paper for very
     Advanced Students
124 Jennifer, the ex J.P.
     answers your
     questions
126 Proof Positive
128 Over-Night
130 Stamping It Out
131 Noting Brief
134 Knowing
137 Roundabout
138 Stafford and Luvaglio

139 Criminal Law Review –
     Some New
     Suggestions
141 Rustling
142 Relieved
143 The Letter
144 Sentencing
147 Bigamy
148 Conspiracy and Too
     Many Charges
149 A Peep into the Jury
     Room
151 Contingency Fees
152 Treasure Trove
157 Judge Jeffreys — Jeffreys
     of the Bloody Assize
158 St Peter and Me
160 Financial Report
161 The Stockbroker's Letter
162 Confessors of all
     Religions in English
     Law

Cartoons by MAC appear on pages vi, 17, 41, 52, 100, 122

Talk

The solicitors had instructed me several times for paper-work, but never in Court. One day the senior partner was in chambers and asked my faithful Clerk Clement if I 'could talk.' Clement burst out laughing. 'Talk', he said, 'our trouble is to stop him talking!' After that they became one of our best Court clients.

The senior partner met Clem one day and said to him, 'Remember that conversation we had? You were dead right. We've just had a case in the Court of Appeal where he wasn't called on – and he was very annoyed!'

The Paternity Suit

When I was a very young barrister I was briefed at a guinea a time by a Catholic Legal Aid Centre rejoicing in the splendid name of The Society of Good Counsel situated in a tiny office in Maiden Lane off the Strand.

One of my first cases for them – one of my first cases ever – was to defend a young man (25) on a paternity claim at a Magistrate's Court.

I met my client and felt he was splendid – I felt all my clients were splendid in those days. I would fight for him to the very end.

The girl (20) I instinctively disliked. Her corroborating witnesses (which included a doctor) too. I put everything into the case.

I called the defendant. He struck me as a superb witness and I believed everything he said. He told how he had met her once, for ten minutes, at a party. At this there were cries of oohs from the other side.

Under cross examination he did not yield an inch.

I addressed the magistrate in a then good Irish accent.

I felt personally very affronted and dismayed when he said 'Case proved.' He called my man forward to ask him about his means. Whereupon my 25 year old said, 'Make it light, Sir, I already have three affiliation orders to pay.'

1

'Who are You?'

It was at Brentford County Court that I fledged my legal wings, before Judge Tudor Rees. Mostly on hire-purchase (everybody in those days seemed to have everything on the 'Never – Never', bitterly disputed small debts and the swarm of possession (eject-ment) cases which followed the 1939-45 War.

It was an unconventional Court. Odd things happened. For example the learned judge gave a donkey 12 months to surrender his stall. It was cut on appeal to something like a month. In cases whose litigants were being hard pressed he would suddenly adjourn the case 'for three months, for further evidence.' There never was any further evidence. On occasions he ordered debtors under hire-purchase agreements to pay the current sum and 10p off the arrears each week and adjourned the case generally.

When one counsel protested to him that such an order would mean that it would take over 100 years to pay off the arrears he said quietly, 'Yes, that's about right.' A lady who admitted to arrears in some 25 hire-purchase agreements was ordered to pay 5p off the arrears on each but 'to go round your things – or rather their things – and choose what you can return if you have to.'

On Rent Act cases for a tenant, one's duty was to amass as much 'hardship' as one could, crippled husband, sickly wife, delicate children, if possible an aged grandfather or senile grand-mother; alternatively just beside husband's work, near the wife's part-time job, convenient for the schools. One judge, at Croydon, virtually conducted these cases himself by having the two parties sworn together and then saying in turn to each, 'Health of family?', 'How many in your family?', 'Any grand-parents or suffering aunts?.'

I learnt many long-held lessons in Judge Tudor-Rees' Court. He was a kind and gentle person to newly-called barristers. I remember best one incident which occurred to me in my youth and – thankfully – was never repeated again. A formidable lady of middle-age was appearing in person to claim possession of the flat from my client, the tenant, for her own occupation. She spoke strongly and vehemently to the judge for about fifteen minutes. Then she said, 'That is my evidence.'

2

I had a lot to ask her – why was she moving from her present flat? What was going to happen to it? How many premises did she own? Had she a cottage in the country? What were her means? Why had she let the flat to my client in the first place?

I rose to cross-examine and before I had uttered a word she turned on me. 'Who are you?', she said with marked hostility.

Again before I could utter a word she said, 'I can't think why you're interfering. Sit down and mind your own business.'

The judge interrupted gently. 'That's the barrister who's going to cross-examine you. Just listen to his questions and answer them.'

'Why should I? I don't want to be whatever you call it.'

'Cross-examined.'

'Yes. I've said what I want to say to you, judge, and I'm not answering anybody else's questions.'

'But he represents the other side and he's entitled to ask you questions.'

'Who says so?'

'I do.'

'Why?'

'I've got to hear both sides of the matter.'

'But this man,' she said, 'knows nothing about it. He's never been in either flat.'

'Have you ever been in Court before or read about trials?'

'No I haven't.'

'You see if this gentleman cross-examines you, you can cross-examine the defendant if he is called.'

'I don't want to. I've told you the truth and you're the one that counts.'

'If I order you to be cross-examined will you answer his questions?'

'But I don't know him, I've never met him. What is he? Who is he?'

'Look, Madam, we've been into all this before. Otherwise I'll have to dismiss your case.'

'That wouldn't be fair', she said. 'I'd have to go to a higher Court.'

'Mr Comyn,' said the judge, 'can you help about this?'

I said with the brashness of youth, 'I don't really want to in view of what Your Honour has said about dismissing this lady's case – but would it not be a good idea for me to put my client's case to you and for you to question her on it? She's obviously not on speaking terms with me.'

'I don't know if she'll speak to me any more, but I'll try your suggestion.'

'Madam', he said, 'will you answer some questions of mine?'

'But hearing you talk you'll only be relaying questions of his.'

'Yes – but they're coming from me and I have a duty to put them.'

'I don't know why but alright I'll answer them.'

I then put to the judge paragraph by paragraph the defence and he questioned her on each. On awkward questions she invariably said, 'What has this got to do with it?', but on the whole she was truthful – and she lost, on the merits.

Too much Turkey

There was heavy frost and snow on the ground, so that no press were in Court, having found out by telephone that there was nothing there to interest them. On the other hand the Circuit Court judge, usually a pleasure to appear before, was in a foul mood. His car had skidded into a ditch on the way to Court and he had suffered a badly sprained ankle. In addition he had broken both lenses of his spectacles. He cursed the cars who wouldn't stop and was given a lift by a friendly coal merchant who let him out at the judge's entrance.

John Brown, the accused, had a name which nobody would pay much attention to until they were told that he was Brown of the national supermarkets, Brownsell.

The judge, by reason of his ankle and broken spectacles, had to be helped on to the bench by his faithful clerk, Hitchin. Nevertheless he stumbled on the step leading to the bench and immediately blamed unfortunate Hitchin. Both counsel in the case sympathised with the judge at the news of his accident. 'Thank

4

you, gentlemen', he said morosely, 'but work must go on, call the first case.'

John Brown then pleaded guilty to stealing and receiving a large turkey cock on December 23rd last.

'I've never heard of these two charges being joined together,' snapped His Lordship. 'It's usually one thing or the other.'

Prosecuting counsel explained. 'He killed the turkey with his car, My Lord, and then took it home and had it for his Christmas dinner.'

'Good Heavens,' remarked the judge, 'cannibalism!'

Anxious to be fair prosecuting counsel said, 'He didn't do it on purpose.'

'What do you mean? Kill the turkey or eat it? I've never heard of anything so monstrous. It's quite appalling. Are the press here? It ought to be widely publicised – everyone would be nauseated.'

'They couldn't get here because of the weather, My Lord.'

'Some of us did. You all did. And I got here – under great difficulty.'

Prosecuting counsel then outlined the facts. The turkey cock belonged to an old widow of 80 who supplemented her income by rearing fowl. This turkey cock – known as Ferdinand – had just become over-all champion at the County Bird Competition and was worth at least £100. The defendant, owner of a chain of supermarkets, was driving home two days before Christmas.'

'What sort of car was it?'

'A Rolls-Royce, My Lord.'

'I thought so. Belongs to his company no doubt.'

There was no word from the defence. Everything possible belonged to the company – even his home.

'The cock was on the road but so were a lot of cocks and hens.'

'It's not being suggested that the cock was negligent!', said the judge provocatively.

'Oh no,' replied counsel, 'after all Mr Brown has pleaded guilty to both charges.'

'You tell me he owns a chain of supermarkets. Presumably he could get a turkey free at one of his stores, instead of running off with this lady's pet bird.'

'I assume so.'

5

'You told me it was Champion at the County Show. How many birds were competing?'

'I understand 86, My Lord.'

'86! And he was Over-All Champion.'

'Yes, over all birds. Ducks, geese, hens, the lot.'

'But £100 is ridiculous for such a bird. Every poulterer and butcher in the county would want it. I'd be inclined to treble it, and then of course she has been out of her money for two months, and no doubt gave it lots of pellets, or whatever you do, for a long time before.'

'Yes, My Lord. The lady was in her cottage and heard brakes screeching and muffled squawks. She ran out and found the defendant putting the cock – on a daily paper – at the back of his car.'

'Not still alive I hope.'

'I'm afraid so.'

'That makes it all the more awful. Stealing an outstanding bird! And having the considerable foresight of putting a paper under it in case it damaged the Rolls. It's almost unbelievable.'

'He made no effort to find the owner. Just drove off with the bird. But she had time to see his number plate and the type of car and she reported it to the garda next day. Two days after Christmas they interviewed the defendant at his house, and he confessed everything including – including the turkey cock, eating it first on Christmas Day and cold on St Stephen's Day.'

'What!' said the judge, 'Not satisfied with one single meal one day he guzzled into it again next day. It's a perfectly awful story. And I suppose day after day. You ought to have included further charges but I'll bear them in mind.'

Prosecuting counsel concluded by saying, 'He has no previous convictions. A man of good character in every way. Aged 68, unmarried. Started life as an assistant butcher in Dublin.'

'Assistant butcher – how appropriate,' echoed the judge. Then he turned to Archic Murphy, defending Mr Brown. 'What do you say – what can you say – about this awful business, Mr Murphy?'

'My client is extremely sorry for what happened.'

'He wasn't at the time, nor when he was taking the second helping on St Stephen's Day.'

'It was all due to a complete lack of judgment. He couldn't help hitting the turkey and having done so he panicked and tried to hide it. He had no intention of eating it. He didn't know where to put it.'

'Into his stomach – Mr Murphy. Into his stomach.'

'One thing led to another, My Lord. He had no idea of eating it until his housekeeper had it plucked and trussed. He hadn't told her how he got it.'

'It's like a case of a farmer stealing a cow.'

'That can't be said about the accident. He drove on because he found a whole lot of turkeys surrounding him.'

'And he picked out the best.'

'They're always the best when they're killed or injured,' said Mr Murphy sadly. 'Never the sickly ones.'

'Why didn't he look for the owner?'

'He didn't know where to find her. Everybody there seemed to have roaming turkeys.'

'Why didn't he try the first cottage he saw?'

'He couldn't see one. Her cottage doesn't front the road and is surrounded by hedges. Also it was late December.'

'But it must have a gate and a drive.'

'Well yes, but he didn't notice them.'

'Didn't want to see them.'

'That's not quite fair, My Lord. There were lots of other cottages nearby and lots of turkeys.

'Why not leave a message with somebody telling what happened and ask them to inform the owner that she would be compensated?'

'It's a good idea now but on the spur of the moment Mr Brown did not think of it.'

'Two, perhaps even three or four, full helpings of a plump turkey cock, (we don't know), for free and illegally. Isn't that greed?'

'No. My client receives many thousands of pounds a year and has a large holding of shares in his company.'

'Something for nothing appeals to that sort of person.'

'He can pay a substantial fine and compensate the woman, though I think with respect that the figure you have suggested for compensation is too much.'

7

'Who said it was going to be a fine?', asked the judge.

A particularly stony silence descended on the Court. Nobody had thought of it until he did, and he was the person who mattered.

A usually loquacious Mr Murphy was struck dumb.

'Say 6 months imprisonment on each charge – 12 months in all. No – perhaps 12 months for deceiving the owner and an additional 6 months for the eating.'

'My Lord, My Lord, there's nothing in his record, nothing.'

'There soon will be, Mr Murphy. Indelibly! These are repulsive matters. Anyway looking at him I can see that a year (or two) on a strict diet with no helpings of turkey, should knock him into shape. And some exercise, after all that turkey.'

Mr Murphy tried again but was finally quietened when the judge said that he was now thinking of a total of perhaps three years.

He retired 'to consider the sentence' and was helped down by Hitchin. Mr Brown was taken down and introduced for the first time to a narrow, white-washed cell, which he hated.

The judge was out for half an hour. When he came back he said, 'Stand up, Mr Hitchin, I propose to sentence you.' The Clerk nearly fainted and there was consternation in Court.

'I beg your pardon, My Lord, it's Mr Brown.'

'Ah yes, Mr Brown, you have pleaded guilty to two quite dreadful offences. Sufficient to put you in jail – a long pause – for a considerable time. At one stage I was thinking of 3 years but it has lessened. (A long pause). But I think you have learnt a lesson, so I can fine you. You will pay £500 in respect of each charge within one month, six months in 'default.' You will pay the owner £300 on the same terms. And you will pay the costs. Have I got power to forbid him keeping or eating turkeys again, Mr Registrar?'

'No, My Lord.'

As the judge left Court Mr Brown sighed – with relief. When Mr Murphy suggested an appeal to him he shook his head violently. 'No, no, no,' he said, 'nothing like this again.' He invited Mr Murphy and his solicitor to lunch ('I'll pay this time') and they went to Jury's Hotel just opposite. 'I do appreciate what you've done', he said. After a couple of gins and tonics all felt better and they went into lunch.

8

The head waiter came up to Mr Brown confidentially. 'I can specially recommend the roast turkey, Sir.' A glimpse of fear came over Mr Brown's face. 'No thank you,' he said, 'I've had enough turkey to last me for ever.'

Doctor X

Although it all happened a long time ago I have had to disguise the facts considerably to protect the man and woman concerned.

I was briefed on behalf of Doctor X leading a colleague from chambers to defend the doctor on five charges of indecent assault upon a woman patient, before the General Medical Council.

He was a married man in his middle forties and carried on his practice as a heart specialist (I have changed his speciality) in a large town in the North of England, which I will call Dunraven. He was the leading heart specialist in the town and probably in the whole of Northern England.

He was well-known throughout the area and had a very high reputation with his colleagues and the public. There had always been universal praise for him up to this, and no sort of criticism. He had two boys, both reading medicine.

The complainant was a woman of about 42, married for years but having no children. Her husband had a responsible position in the town and she did not go out to work.

From the formal pre-trial document we learnt that she said that she had been referred to Doctor X by her local G.P. for some long-standing trouble and that she had attended him on seven occasions. Nothing out of the ordinary had happened over the first two, but on the other five he had touched her and fondled her quite inappropriately and made lewd suggestions to her. It was only after the third occasion that she had complained – to her local G.P. He said in effect that she was reading too much into what a strange doctor had done. On the fifth occasion he went further than before and again there were lewd suggestions.

We also learnt that she had then complained to her husband, who forbade her to go any more.

9

Also she ominously complained that on the telephone after she had lodged the complaint, Doctor X had rung her up and asked what mortgage they had on the house and when she replied 'about £4,000' he had said that he would pay if off if she dropped the case. But she refused.

We had two long consultations with the doctor before the case. He was adamant in his denial of the charges alleged.

'She came back to me seven times,' he said, 'and she never made one word of complaint. My secretary was in the next room, she made no complaint to her and at the end simply made another appointment with me.'

'Do you think it could all be attributed to the menopause?,' I asked.

'I suppose it could be,' he said. 'Strange things do happen in the menopause but I must say I've never heard of this sort of allegation arising out of it.'

'How many women do you treat a year, Doctor?'

'Just over half my patients are women,' he replied, 'say about three hundred.'

'All ages?'

'No. Mostly from about the early twenties to the middle sixties. That's when the trouble affects them.'

'Any complaints from any of them?'

'None at all – except occasional remarks that my treatment didn't seem to be doing them much good.'

'You never had a nurse in your surgery when you treated women?'

'Never. I'm afraid I belong to the old school.'

'Now, Doctor, what about this allegation that you phoned up and offered to pay off their mortgage if she dropped the charges?'

'That's quite right,' he replied. 'It was a foolish thing to do, I realise now. But these cases are heard in open court with free press coverage and it was worth anything to me to get out of them. It wasn't meant as any kind of admission of guilt.'

'Did you ask your wife before you did it?' asked my junior.

'No. I know she wouldn't have approved. I told her sometime later and though she didn't approve she understood.'

We discussed the allegations in detail and then discussed the likely witnesses to call. His wife, as to their happy married life; his secretary; two witnesses as to character, one medical and one lay; and if possible the G.P.

At the second consultation we heard two things of importance. One that made it very debatable that we should call the G.P. He had told our instructing solicitor that she was very distressed when she had called on him and was very explicit in her allegations – but she had not, definitely had not, said anything at all about lewd suggestions. He had not so far been asked to give evidence for the woman. Secondly we heard from the Doctor that there has been persistent rumours in the area that a certain national newspaper had offered her a very large sum for three or four articles – if he was found guilty. There was no reliable information as to the sum (£25,000 had been mentioned vaguely) or as to whether she had signed a contract or not.

The trial before the committee (with its Legal Assessor) lasted for three days and unfortunately attracted particular press coverage, with photographs of the parties, of their houses and of the witnesses.

I was fairly hopeful of the result. There was not much corroboration, she had gone on visiting.

She was the first witness. Far from attractive in appearance, quiet and timid in speech, commendably brief in her answers, but – as I thought – overshy and over-hesitant in her reply to the vital questions, and feigning distress and near tears as required.

In cross-examination such a witness requires very careful handling. Gentle, quiet, an occasional touch of sympathy but always a glimpse of hardness and disbelief. Also questions to throw her off her guard by unexpected ones and questions taken out of sequence.

When I rose to cross-examine I paused for a good half minute before starting – to let everyone see how she reacted to this tasking part of the case.

'Tell us, Mrs Y, do you resent the press publicity this case is receiving?' She paused and then said, 'I do.'

'Did you know when you brought it that it would attract such publicity?'

'No.'

11

'Do you like publicity?'

'Of course not.'

'I'm going to read out the names of nine daily and national newspapers and ask you if any of them have been in contact with you.' I then read out slowly the names of the papers. 'Well, Mrs Y?'

She looked at me suspiciously, paused and said, 'Three of them have been in touch with me, yes.'

'What to do?'

'For a story from me.'

'If Dr. X was found guilty?'

'Yes.'

'Who offered you the most?'

'The Fleet Street Echo.'

'How much?'

She dropped her voice as she said, '£40,000.'

'Have you accepted it?'

'My own solicitor is dealing with it.'

'On the basis that if you win you get all, if you lose you get nothing?'

'Something like that.'

'And you said you resented publicity, didn't you?'

There was no answer. 'Why didn't you take the offer Doctor X made to pay off your mortgage?'

'I wouldn't touch any of his money.'

'Not enough?' She glared at me but did not reply.

'You knew it wasn't a confession, just an effort to buy you off?'

'I took it as a confession.'

'Why have you taken these proceedings against him?'

'To expose him.'

'You realise they will ruin him even if he wins?'

'I don't care.'

My instructing solicitor had done a lot of good work and I was able to confront her with nine running complaints over the past four years – against the Railway, the Highway Authority, the Electricity Board, the Gas Board, Telecom etc., all to no avail.

I then had to go into details about her allegations against the Doctor about which she remained firm; as to why she had made no protests to the secretary at the time and just fixed another appointment. She was notably weak; as to why she had taken up the other appointments (on which she was again weak); and as to the rather belated complaints she made ('I was very distressed and shy about them').

Next she called her G.P. He was firmer in his evidence on her side than we had expected but, although she was obviously very upset, there were no tears and no mention of nasty expressions. Relieved that we did not call him, I asked him very few questions.

Her husband was a good witness. He spoke of an ideally happy marriage, of the complaints she made and that he had always found her fair and trustworthy. Under cross-examination by me he agreed that he had not heard before about her complaints to the Public Services ('but she does react strongly to being unjustly treated'), and he agreed, rather reluctantly that selling her story to a newspaper was against his advice. 'We argued about it,' he said, 'but she said there would be publicity anyway and it was an awful lot of money. The choice was hers.'

She finally called two women friends to say that she was a perfectly normal person, in no way aberrational about sex and never given to dirty language or jokes.

I submitted No Case To Answer in respect of all counts, on the footing that there was insufficient evidence and corroboration. The committee withdrew for ten minutes and came back to say that they were against me.

We immediately called the doctor, his wife, the secretary and the two character witnesses.

He was a good and firm witness. Under a rigid cross-examination he never faltered, except that he was not as strong about paying off the mortgage as he could have been.

His wife was too emotional and angry to be a good witness. The secretary was excellent and the character witnesses all that we wanted.

Came the final speeches. The committee rose and were out for over an hour and a half. They brought their legal adviser in twice.

Each charge was read out. Not Guilty – Not Guilty – Not Guilty – Not Guilty; and then quite unexpectedly to us (and I think the crammed courtroom) to the fifth charge – Guilty.

I got up immediately and said that there would of course be an appeal against 'this inconsistent finding.' I addressed them shortly on mitigation. They retired for a few minutes. When they came back the chairman said, 'Doctor X will be struck off the Register.' Somewhat impertinently, I asked, 'For a period or indefinitely?' The chairman said 'Indefinitely.'

We adjourned to chambers to puzzle out this odd verdict. My Junior came up with the best 'explanation' – that all except two had no corroboration; that they did not rely on the G.P.; but on the fifth charge they accepted that she had corroborated everything to her husband.

'But,' I asked, 'wouldn't that corroborate all the charges?'

'No,' he replied, 'It wouldn't be sufficiently close in time for the others.'

We appealed. But it was not long before I found that we were facing difficulty.

One of Their Lordships said, 'You called this a curious and unsatisfactory case, Mr. Comyn. But is it not open to the committee to reject four charges and find the facts against you on the fifth?'

'It's surely extraordinary,' I replied. 'It looks inconsistent and is surely illogical and unsafe.'

Another of Their Lordships said, 'When I was a trial judge I had quite a few cases of apparently conflicting verdicts but they were upheld on Appeal because no one knew what motivated the jury – maybe for example giving the benefit of the doubt to the accused.'

'But this committee,' I said, 'basically had to decide which party was telling the truth and if they could not accept her word on the first four how could they on the fifth?'

'Perhaps they found sufficient corroboration there.'

'But,' I said, 'that would have corroborated the whole.'

I continued my argument without any significant interruption for the whole of that day and into the next. Even if these two judges were against me there were three others.

As I was coming to the end of my speech the chairman made an observation – which I find appalling in far too many Appeal Courts – 'Even if we might have decided differently, how can we interfere?' I said, 'That with respect is a wholly dangerous argument in a grave case. What are Appeal Courts for but to review a whole case – in depth?'

One of the earlier Law Lords said, 'We normally do not interfere with findings of fact, Mr. Comyn, unless they are plainly wrong.'

'There seems,' I said, 'little point in having an Appeal system if it will not act when it is concerned or doubtful about it – where it might have been decided differently by Your Lordships.'

The appeal was dismissed – 'for reasons to be given later.'

I addressed a few observations on penalty but was met by the finding that that was for the committee to decide (why?) and they would not interfere.

After the appeal the woman's story appeared in four successive editions of the paper. It told in edited version the whole of her story, but there was nothing to be gained by libel proceedings.

The doctor returned home. After two years we applied for him to be restored to the register – and he was. He soon built up as successful a practice as before.

I think few believed her except those who mattered.

Do Judges remember? — Do Judges Regret?

A judge's sentence is not official until he has certified it at the end of his session and I know a few judges who have pronounced one sentence in Open Court (in terrorem) but lowered it in their Official Record.

There was on Old Bailey judge, Judge Alan King Hamilton QC, who fined a company I represented in a building fraud case one million pounds. That was on a Tuesday. On the Friday afternoon his clerk rang and asked for prosecuting counsel and myself to be in Court on the Monday morning. He then said, in Open Court, 'Having reflected on this case I believe that my fine was too high and I propose to reduce it to £750,000. 'He had arranged for the Press to be there 'because the case attracted some public attention and I would like it to be as widely known that I have changed my mind.' A most admirable feature all round. Another judge, Mr Justice Stable, would on a suitable occasion mischievously bargain with you about a suitable sentence. On one occasion he said to me, 'Alright, Mr Comyn, let's split the difference – nine months.' And they talk about the faults of plea-bargaining!

There was an Assize judge on the Western Circuit, Mr Justice Brabin I think it was, who sent for me the morning after I had lost a personal injuries action before him and said, 'I've been worrying about that case ever since. I think I was wrong, completely wrong. You must appeal it.' We did, and we won.

The late Mr Justice Thesiger pretended that he put right out of his mind every case, however gruesome, once he had finished with it. I remember two occasions of lunching beside him at The Inner Temple (by necessity rather than by design) and he disclaimed all memory of a memorable murder trial (where my young client was hanged) and of an appalling diminished responsibility case where a man had stabbed his mother some thirty times. He always appeared to have the air of perpetual infallibility.

Mr Justice Melford Stevenson, a caustic judge in and out of Court, did not like Mr Justice Thesiger, and when I was going to cite a reported decision of the Court he kept trying to put me off. But I persisted and Melford said wearily 'Alright. Let's see what contribution to English jurisprudence he made on this occasion.'

Melford had an extremely good memory for his cases. I recall somebody asking him if he regretted any of his decisions. 'Oh yes', he said. 'Two in the last month in fact.' He mentioned two cases where he had given prisoners thirty years. 'I wish now I had added another.

There was a rude and bad-tempered judge, with a memory like a sieve except for his own rudeness, who was often extremely nasty to my Master in the Law, Edward Holroyd Pearce, and others. When Edward Holroyd Pearce was in Court before him on one occasion he happened to say, 'But of course Your Lordship knows more about ship-building than I do.' Whereupon the judge said, 'I know more about everything than you do, Mr Pearce.' He was thankfully a very rare phenomenon on the Bench. I remember drawing him on one of my first cases in the High Court and asking

16

my devoted Clerk, Clem, if he would add 'danger money' to my fee!

A judge whom it was quite unpredictable to appear before was Lord Merriman, one of the last Presidents of that ill-assorted Court, the Probate, Divorce and Admiralty Division, before it became the Family Division. He prided himself – quite inaccurately – on an outstanding memory and perfect hearing.

There was a morning when I think it was John Mortimer and I turned up to hear a reserved (deferred) judgment of his in a case. It soon transpired that it was in a completely different case. Efforts to tell him so by his clerk and the registrar met with irritable waving of his hand and he went on to the end. Then finding that there were no solicitors or counsel in the case he upbraided them for not being in Court.

Then he noticed me in Court and asked sharply why we were there. 'To mention Collins deceased', we said.

'Never heard of it', he replied.

I tried to remind him. At last he said, 'Ah yes, it's coming back to me. My mind was still occupied with the last case. Yes, yes, it

'We'll let him go another five miles then nab him for kerb-crawling.'

was about a woman jockey who made her Will in a train, or perhaps died in a train.'

Getting support from my opponent I said, very diffidently, 'I thought she was a lady solicitor.'

'Maybe, maybe. But I know she was in a train at some certain stage.'

'Probably was,' I said cautiously. After all most people take trains.

'I rather thought she wrote the will in her partner's office.'

'No, I think you're wrong about that. Anyway it's a very difficult case and I haven't made up my mind about it. Come back three weeks today and I'll give judgment.'

On occasions the learned President would say. 'I've been referred to many cases but I think the law is best expressed in some words of my own in cvd. I will read it.' Then he did so with loving care and obvious approval.

In a case called *Simpson v Simpson* before the President everyone calculated it as a halfday's case. He decided to turn it into a leading case on cruelty and it lasted for fifteen further days. It meant that our arrangements in Chambers were blown sky high because no less than three of us had to devise parts of the case for each other – Roger Ormrod and Robin Dunn (both later Lord Justices) and myself.

The President had certain favourite phrases. One was 'The less I say about this case the better' – followed by an hour's Judgment. Another was 'Since we are sending this case back for a re-trial I want to make it abundantly plain that we are not seeking to fetter them in any way' and followed by three quarters of an hour of close fettering.

Mr Justice Hilbery had a memory like an elephant – and could squirt water over counsel too. Not taking many notes he could recall them much later, word for word, some phrase or question they had put forward which now embarrassed them. He was a tall, stern, unsmiling man, whose views you could tell from his face and who certainly thought he was never wrong or ever regretted anything. In an infant case where I was asking approval for a settlement he turned to my opponent and said 'Mr Everett what superfluity of munificence has overcome you! Go away and strain yourself to even greater bounty'.

There were two judges – Mr Justice Avery and Mr Justice Humphreys, 'The Hanging Judges', who were of the Hilbery mould. When I first knew them they had faces of old dried parchment and low but very audible voices, which stung. They seemed to have no emotion; if they had they concealed it well.

Lord Goddard, Lord Chief Justice, had a face which he could turn into a growl but was a man of a good deal of humanity at heart. I seemed to get a harsher time from him in the Court of Criminal Appeal when I had his grand-daughter as a pupil! One incident was when I was rising to open an appeal against sentence and he barked and said, 'Well, Mr Comyn, what's wrong with this very lenient sentence?'

On another occasion, when I was eventually on my feet, he said, 'What did he get for all this?'

'Two years My Lord.'

'Good Heavens,' he said.

He had an excellent memory and I would certainly say regretted nothing.

Lord Denning, Master of the Rolls for many years, had an encyclopaedic knowledge of his own cases and the law generally. He was a reformer par excellence. When frequently overruled by the House of Lords he showed no regret of any kind and seemed to wish that he had gone further on and he soon attempted to.

Mr Justice Wallington was an irascible judge of the Probate, Divorce and Admiralty Division. He frightened litigants – and counsel. I was present one day in Court when a woman witness had just been sworn and he was looking for papers. She leant over to have a close-up view of this man she had heard talking so much. He found his papers, switched round and found her staring at him. 'What do you think you're doing, madam?', whereupon she fainted. Everybody was in a great fuss, except the judge, who said, 'Counsel, call your next witness.'

I remember many, many, kind and pleasant High Court and County Court judges. One was Mr Justice Morris (later Lord Morris). One day I was waiting to come on before him. I looked into Court two or three times and found him trying a case conducted in person by two belligerent litigants. When I first went in they and their supporters were conducting an all-round consultation. Next time I went in the kind and courteous judge had restored them to some kind of order. When I went in before lunch to see how things were going I heard him, about to adjourn, saying gently to each side, 'Would ten minutes to two be alright for you?' and 'For you, would ten minutes to two be alright for you?'

There was another judge who was tactlessly reminded by a colleague of an Appeal from him which had just been allowed and asked him who the Court were. 'Let me see,' said the judge, 'ah yes – the two Smiths and a proper judge.'

Another was asked much the same question and replied, 'A weak Court, my deal fellow, a damned weak Court.'

I have said enough to answer the questions put at the beginning. Yes – I think nearly all judges remember their cases. And No – I think most of them have no regrets for what they have done or said. It is not, it would seem, a game for post-mortems.

Speaking personally, I worried a lot about cases while I was trying them, but not after Judgment. I occasionally had regrets, usually as to whether I had stressed something sufficiently. It is not so much an air of omnipotence that falls round a judge but an air of conclusiveness and inevitability ('There it is. What I've said, I've said').

Relegated

In 1972 the Crown Court came into existence, replacing Assizes and Quarter Sessions by a three-tier Court consisting of the High Court Judge's Court, the Circuit Judge's Court and the Recorder's Court (that of a part-time judge). Many crimes were inter-changeable.

On one occasion I was sitting as Recorder at Exeter. A man who was up for a series of thefts was listed for hearing before the High Court judge on Monday – but was not reached; again on Tuesday, but again not reached. Transferred to the Circuit judge's list the same thing happened on both Wednesday and Thursday. He was then put in my list as recorder for the Friday. After a day's hearing he was convicted and I sentenced him to five months, bearing in mind he had been in custody for three months awaiting trial.

Later on his counsel told me of a good remark he made. On hearing on the Friday morning that he was now in my list he said, 'God streuth: from the First Division to the Third in one bloody week.

Spy Cases

I defended in eight Spy cases while I was at the Bar. Two were successful, in two we pleaded Not Guilty but were convicted, and in the other four it was a plea of Guilty and mitigation. The standard sentence appeared to be 21 years. Blake got 42 years but escaped later.

In one case at Winchester I defended a naval Sub-Lieutenant for spying for the Russians. We pleaded Guilty and got 21 years. It was really a most amateur affair. The favourite pick-up points were large stones carved out and a message or documents put inside, the whole placed on the site of different County Council stone heaps.

In North Wales I defended a pilot-officer for attempting to sell secrets of the Hurricanes to the Russians. He pleaded Not Guilty but was convicted and got 21 years. This was again a very amateur affair. He was under suspicion and was secretly photographed approaching the Russian Embassy, then going in and coming out.

The case of Nicholas Prager brought me up to Leeds, once again against my old opponent, the then Attorney-General, Sir Peter Rawlinson (now Lord Rawlinson).

An extraordinary thing happened to me the night before the case. It was about 1.30 am and I was reading in bed. I had the door locked because of the documents I had. Suddenly the door opened and a Fleet Street journalist I knew (one of the few I never liked) came in and said, 'Make it worth your while if you tell me what Prager is going to plead in the morning. A good scoop for us.'

I said, 'Get to hell out of here this instant.'

He replied, 'Steady on. Let me talk to you.'

'No,' I said, 'I'm going to ring the police and have you arrested,' and despite his physical efforts to prevent me, I did so. I did not trust the downstairs staff; where else could he have got the key?

The police arrived and I told them what had happened and identified the man. 'It's pretty serious,' said the Inspector, 'especially with you having secret papers.'

'I know you'll use your own discretion with him, Inspector, but be light with him if you can. He's just a boozy old hack journalist. Perhaps an arrest and a good talking-to might do the trick.'

Prager pleaded Not Guilty to eight charges of spying for the Russians via the Czechs. The charges related to ten years before when he was in the RAF and included principally all his disclosure of the radar scanning equipment in the RAF's V-bombers.

He came from a Czech background (his father naturalised British) and he had a Czech wife. The Crown alleged that after he came to England he joined the RAF on false information. Very strangely he got through the RAF 'vetting' and was posted to high secret work, which brought him into touch with the anti-radar equipment.

We had our difficulties but there were points in our favour – a ten year delay, good reports from the RAF and his present employment and that the Crown would be calling informers and defectors, whom Juries as a rule dislike and distrust. Prager also had his own individual defence, a complete denial plus an attack that anything suspicious was attributable to his wife and an RAF friend of hers.

The Crown called their informer and defectors, who were good but obviously did not please the jury. The Court went into camera to hear their evidence.

After a very long adjournment the jury returned a verdict of Guilty on three counts and Not Guilty on one. The then Lord Chief Justice, Lord Widgery, gave him twelve years. I believe from conversations afterwards, that the Prosecution and the Security Services regarded it as an extremely serious case and that the sentence was too light. I think it was measured against the ten years delay.

We appealed – unsuccessfully. But the case is an important legal authority for the proposition that 'The Judges rules' are discretionary only and that long length of interview and caution can be disregarded if the statement or statements are truly voluntary. That is what the chief held when I made my submissions to him on the point. I remember saying to him, 'Why Rules if they Rule nothing?'

The Surveyor

£10,000 he charged for the model! £10,000 and being multi-millionaires they paid without question. The solicitors were their standing solicitors– (they didn't really have to stand for anyone else) and were obviously magnificently paid. Counsel were as usual grossly underpaid.

It was a planning application for the company's vast Headquarters in the West End of London. They wanted, quite naturally, to being its 18th century facade up to 20th century standards.

We had numerous consultations with the clients, the well-known surveyor and his solicitor. He kept telling me of his successes, which seemed to make him both Top Of The League and Cup Champion for years in a row. He exuded optimism.

At the eve of trial consultation he produced with triumph, and the help of two assistants, the Model. What it was going to look like. Large, heavy and impressive.

Everybody admired it – except my Junior.

'Mr X,' he said, 'in one of their early letters didn't the Ministry say they wanted a building which was vertical and not horizontal? Your model is entirely horizontal.'

There was momentary silence. Then the Great Man spoke, 'I'd forgotten that. But not to worry – we'll verticalise it over night.'

Next morning I opened the case before the Inspector – a brisk stand-no-nonsense man of about 50. There were surprisingly few objections; chiefly neighbours worried about dust, undue noise and scaffolding.

I naturally opened with the Ministry letter and said 'We have produced that model over there accordingly.'

He glanced at it and said 'I've been to examine the site three times.' I nodded my commendation.

'What struck me,' he went on, 'is that it needs another storey to bring it level with other buildings.' Struck him – we were all thunder-struck.

'Moreover,' he said, 'I would like to see it turned around so that the entrance was put in the side-street.'

I gulped. The clients gulped. The surveyor had horror written on his face.

'Then,' said the Inspector, 'I would like two end windows on all four sides blocked up with the same stone.'

'Also,' he went on, ' a flat roof not a coned, slated roof.'

'And finally,' he said, 'I would like the name of your company spread all along the top, not just put on a brass plate by the door.'

'But, but,' I said, 'it would need altering the whole inside.'

'That doesn't matter,' he said.

'We'd have to close down the place for years.'

'I'm sure they could find Company Headquarters.'

Of my own initiative I asked him for an adjournment indefinitely. We had numerous Consultations. I have never seen top business-men look so worried.

We never went back. The old building is still there – untouched.

The Circus Case

My client was a commercial traveller from Dublin, dealing (of all things) in wine, spirits and beer.

On this particular day he had calls to pay in Trim, County Meath, and then by one of the most circuitous and slowest roads in the country to Kinnegad, about twenty miles away.

He was treated rather too well by his customers in Trim and vowed that he would have nothing but light refreshments in Kinnegad.

He bowled off briskly, perhaps too briskly, for Kinnegad. All went well for half the journey. Then, taking a corner too quickly, he ran into a Circus going the same way as he was.

At the end of the Circus, tied to the others trunk to trunk, was a small elephant. My client tipped him on the tail – his usual sign to sit down – and he promptly sat down on my client's engine bonnet, wrecking it. Sheer curiosity then brought him round to the side, which with a few good thumps he stove in.

The client and the circus owner exchanged particulars and my client was just able to get the car to Kinnegad. There was a Garda on duty at the junction into the town. Seeing this battered vehicle coming towards him he stopped it.

Viewed in retrospect it was unwise of my client to say, 'Not to worry, officer, an elephant sat on my car.'

The officer smelt a whiff of drink and telling him 'to pull in over there' hauled him to the Station. There he repeated his explanation, which was received cooly.

He was brought down to the cells and a police surgeon was sent for. He took a long time to come and my client had sobered up sufficiently to be 'doubtful' on the tests.

Half an hour later the Circus pondered its way into the town. All was explained, all was forgiven.

A wise commercial traveller would have left his car in to be repaired and travelled back to Dublin by train. But not my client. He went off to a local pub, rejoicing. Then he told everybody about the whole incident. There was much jolting and laughing, a number of invitations to have a drink and many visits to see the badly bashed car.

Eventually as evening came the client staggered out back to his car. There was the same policeman as in the morning. He arrested him and brought him once again to the station. There he was charged with being drunk in charge, drunk and disorderly – and having no red lights. After an interval in a cell for sobering up he was released on police bail.

A month later we had a spirited battle before the District Justice at Summerhill, who if not a tee-totaller himself felt that all others should be. We pleaded Not Guilty to being drunk in charge but Guilty to the other two.

He dearly wished to find the client Guilty of being drunk in charge but the client was a good 25 yards from the car when the officer arrested him, and had lost his keys. Very reluctantly he dismissed the charge, adding 'but no costs under any circum-stances'. I turned to the drunk charge and tried to introduce some lightness into the affair by referring to the elephant affair. He was not amused. I tried to make it out as one of the town's most joyful days which unfortunately led to uncustomary over-indulgence.

'Has he been sacked?', asked the District Justice.

'Certainly not, sir. He works for well-known brewers and distillers.'

'Good God! A man with his dispositions.'

He then imposed a fine of £200 on the drink charge and £25 on the no lights summons which was the part that wrangled most with my client. Seven days to pay or a month inside.

Irish Legal Studies

In the days before Independence Tim Healy KC was mocking a decision of the House of Lords which was against him, saying, 'The voice of infallibility appears to have said, by three votes to two, that I am wrong.'

* * * *

On another occasion a King's Bench Judge in Ireland said to counsel, who was about to cite a House of Lords case, 'Don't cite me the decisions of remote judges. Have we any case here at home on the point?'

* * * *

A very youthful barrister in Cork was asked his name by the Usher on behalf of the judge. He said loudly, 'My name is Sam Smith. What's the judge's name?'

* * * *

A rather bellicose barrister at Limerick was cross-examining a gentle old lady. She suddenly lapsed into silence.

'Why don't you answer?', asked the judge in a kindly way.

'I'm frightened of him,' she said.

'And by God so am I,' replied the judge.

* * * *

Two counsel who disliked each other were opponents in The Supreme Court. The counsel who was opening at enormous length was obviously very proud of appearing for a County Board. Frequently he kept saying 'The Board this' and 'The Board that'. Eventually his opponent half rose and said audibly 'B-O-R-E-D I presume'.

* * * *

An elderly judge at the Four Courts had been talking of resigning for some time. But he was back on duty for the next legal year. At lunch a brother judge asked him why. 'Well,' he said, 'when I mentioned it to my wife she threw a fit of hysterics and said, 'My God, having you around all day, every day, is just too much.'

* * * *

There was a judge in County Clare who was very old, grown small and stooped with age. Counsel called a witness equally old and stooped. Mistaking where the witness-box was he began to mount the judge's steps.

'Stop,' said counsel, 'you're not the judge.'

Having a good look at him the witness said, 'Shur I don't think I'm fit for anything else now.

* * * *

'Extraordinary our legal system', said one counsel to another at the Central Criminal Court (Green Street).

'Why?'

'His Lordship has just let the prisoner out on bail and locked up the jury for the night.'

* * * *

'Revenge, Mr Hardy,' said a middle-aged lady, 'yes that's why I'm here – and you're no bad hand at it yourself.'

* * * *

'You will be flogged all the way down the Quays.' said Lord Norbury to a prisoner. 'Thank you, My Lord. You have done your worst.'

'That is only half the sentence,' said the judge, 'and back again.'

* * * *

Carson and his junior once lost a murder trial. The junior said, 'All we can hope for now is a reprieve.'

Referring to the Chief Secretary Carson replied, 'He'd hang his own wife.'

'Yes,' said the junior, 'I've met her and I know what you mean.'

* * * *

A Circuit Court judge in Carlow asked a long-winded counsel how long more he would be, 'Five minutes, My Lord.'

'Good,' said the judge, 'bargain clinched.'

English Legal Stories

Samuel Warren (1807-1872) of the Inner Temple, was the author of the famous legal novel Ten Thousand A Year. He published it anonymously but liked everyone to know who had written it and to have it praised. One day at lunch he asked a colleague if he had read it and what he thought of it.

'Unfair to ask me that, Warren,' said the colleague, 'you see I wrote it.'

* * * *

Warren was many things in his time; a QC, an honorary DCL of Oxford, an MP, writer of legal text-books and novels and finally a Master in Lunacy. But he was also rather a snob. On one occasion he said to a fellow barrister that he had been dining at the Duke of T's house the other evening and to his surprise there was no fish.

'Easy explanation for that,' said his companion, 'they'd eaten it all upstairs.'

* * * *

A barrister left his shoes to be mended twenty years ago at a cobbler's shop near the Temple. He forgot about them but then found the ticket and went into the shop. The lady assistant said, 'Twenty years is a long time. We've changed hands three times since then. But I'll go and see.' She came back a few minutes later and said, 'Should be ready on Friday.'

* * * *

Counsel had flown an aircraft before but wanted to brush up his knowledge in preparation for an Air Enquiry in a fortnight's time. He's a bit old, thought the Training School Manager, but still his documents are in order and so he says has lots of experience; I'll give him one of our best machines.

A few minutes later the aircraft was back on the ground, a jangled tangled wreck. Miraculously the pilot got out of the wreckage completely unharmed.

One of the staff said, 'Was the pilot hurt?'

'No,' said the manager angrily, 'Not yet.'

* * * *

'I'm in a dilemma,' said one elderly barrister to another. 'I've got to send a wedding present on the wedding of my old friend Rothchild's daughter. It would be absurd to give a Rothchild an expensive present. What I want is something not very valuable but which is personal and rare. Can you suggest anything?'

His friend thought for a second and said, 'Why not a lock of your hair?'

* * * *

Two former Lord Chancellors were discovering how they had made their appointments, one said, 'Caeteris paribus I used to appoint my friends.'

To which the other said, 'Damn caeteris paribus.'

* * * *

A lady had given evidence in an assault case at Clerkenwell and was about to call her husband to corroborate when the magistrate said, by way of warning, 'I don't believe a word your wife has said.'

The husband replied, 'That's the difference between us, I have to.'

In the draft of the judge's address to Queen Victoria there occurred the phrase 'Conscious as we are of our own unworthiness for this great office'; Lord Bowen interrupted to say, 'Why not 'Conscious as we are of each others' unworthiness?'

* * * *

30

A witness told Mr Justice Darling that he had been wedded to truth since infancy. 'And when did you become a widower?', asked the judge.

* * * *

A young solicitor was articled to his father. 'Whatever you do,' said father, 'read everything you can about Company Law.'

'Why father?'

'Because it will teach you better than anything else how fraudulent people can be and still stay honest.'

In Admiralty

I was only once 'in Admiralty' – but Thank Goodness never again. A solicitor who knew nothing about shipping briefed one of equal knowledge to apply for adjournment of an Admiralty case, which he thought the other side might agree to.

In the Robing Room I was joking with a friend and 'boasting' of my new excursion into unchartered waters. He put on a solemn face and said, 'Look Jimmy, I've done a little Admiralty work – be sure to ask that whatever order is made be 'attached to the ship's mast'. Very important. It doesn't operate otherwise.'

I thanked him profusely and wrote the magic words down on my Brief.

Outside the Court I met my opponent, who agreed to the adjournment.

I knew the judge slightly and he showed some surprise at seeing a Common Lawyer get up to make an Application in the midst of Admiralty Silks and Juniors waiting to get on with their case.

All went well until I got to the end of my application.

'Very well,' said the judge, 'adjourned generally.'

I looked at my brief to get the words right. 'And would Your Lordship say that your order be attached to the mast of the ship?'

'I beg your pardon,' said His Lordship. I detected notes of disapproval from the Admiralty Bar.

Eventually the judge recovered his breath and turned to my opponent and said, 'What do you say?'

'I didn't know my friend was going to ask for this. It's unique in my experience but if he wants it we have no objection.'

'Well it is exceptional with orders granting an adjournment. Do you really want it?'

I said Yes Please.

'No, Mr Comyn, it isn't necessary and I will refuse it on this occasion.'

As we left Court my solicitor said, 'Will it prejudice our case?'

I said No – the judge doesn't think so. And I went off to find my Robing Room 'friend'.

Sodomy

It was once called 'The Abominable Crime' but now it is lawful in England between 'consenting male adults in private'. With young boys it is very prevalent. Like incest it is very hard to detect and the boys are too frightened to complain. And there are, unfortunately, young male brothels.

Its prevalence is used by many as an argument against boy-only boarding schools, and by others as an argument for priests marrying.

Having had some experience of these cases I am convinced of two things – (1) they know that the Law takes a grave view of their offences but (2) they cannot think why, for to them it is right and natural.

It is not, I believe, a sexual aberration but part of a man's nature. Although there have been many in history who have practised it, it is not natural. The fact that it is practised in secret is due to fear of the Law – and the boy.

I believe it cannot be cured. For one thing, the man does not as a rule want to be cured and will not co-operate. He wants to go on doing what gives him pleasure and satisfaction. It is something which colours his own life and behaviour. Most people in life are able to control their sexual feelings as circumstances

32

demand but there appears to be no such control in the sodomite.

I remember three cases I had particularly well. An were for men of good education, capable of hard work.

One was for a teacher of 10 to 12 years old in a London school; mixed boys and girls. He was in his middle thirties, unmarried and with no previous record. After three years in his job the allegation was that he kept boys back after class and buggered them in the classroom. One boy, who had been given a pound, was asked by his parents where he got it and told the whole story. In Brixton Remand Prison he told me and my junior that it was not a crime, except in the eyes of the Law. I asked him why little boys? He said 'because they are more attractive'. I asked him about corrupting them. He laughed and said most of them are what you call corrupt already. I asked him about women friends and he said he never had any.

My junior asked him how he was going to plead. 'Guilty of course,' he replied, 'the charges are true and I want to spare a lot of the boys giving evidence.'

'You think they might have feelings?'

He said, 'not about the buggery but about giving evidence.' We pressed him on that and he finally agreed that three or four – out of many – had protested 'at first'.

'What do you think the parents would say if they suspected this sort of thing?', asked my junior.

'Doubtless,' he said, 'they have their own sexual problems.'

I pointed out to him that a plea of Not Guilty might succeed in one or two of the charges; boys not attending or being weak on evidence. But he was adamant, he would plead Guilty to all. I made him sign a statement in my brief that these were his own, personal Instructions.

'What will I get, Mr Comyn?', he asked.

'It can only be a guess,' I replied, 'but I would say seven years.'

'With my good record?'

'Yes, you're a teacher you see, in charge of those children.'

'They're not children, you know.'

'To most of us they are,' I replied, 'and to the judge they will be.'

After I had mitigated at the trial, stressing that he had spared the boys giving evidence, the judge said, 'I find this a very difficult case to pass sentence. I would like an opportunity of thinking about it. I will adjourn it until after the mid-day adjournment.'

At two o'clock he came back and after considering the case with great care sentenced him to six years. Some of the newspapers criticised him next day.

I like to know how clients get on afterwards. I heard that this one on release changed his name and went to New Zealand.

The second case was defending a respectable farmer's son of about 40. He was employed in a good position with merchant bankers in the City of London. He lived in a house of his own in one of the suburbs. He had two previous convictions for sodomy, for which he received four and six years' imprisonment respectively. He saw no wrong at all in sodomy with boys of 10 to 14. His prison sentences had taught him nothing at all; except that there were many opportunities of buggery in prison.

As means of getting young boys he advertised under a box number in the local paper, as follows: 'Saturdays and Sundays, young boys or girls (note the word girls) to wash and clean car or to exercise dog. Handsome remuneration.' Crowds came and he chose, discarding all girls.

After a couple of months one boy complained to his parents; he was one of the regulars, one of the favourites. Soon the whole story came out.

I told him that on the documents I had seen there was no defence but he said he was preparing to plead Not Guilty – would I defend him? I said 'Yes' but explained that there were Rules which precluded me suggesting to any boy that he was lying and against me calling him to lie. He said he understood.

We had two consultations in prison before the trial. Then on the third Consultation we had to part company. He insisted that I ask each boy as opening questions 'When were you first buggered? And by whom?'

I, my junior, my solicitor – we all tried to explain to him that I could not put such questions without evidence to support them. Moreover it would betray his whole case, by showing that he was on such terms with these boys as to be able to discuss such a matter with them.

He insisted and in the end defended himself. Found Guilty on all charges he was sentenced to ten years.

The third case concerned a man, who dressed as a cleric, used to meet long-distance trains and buses and pick out three or four 'to help'. They were of both sexes, rather older than the ones I have mentioned, and usually escaping from home. Now rather frightened they enjoyed his friendship and help. The Station staff came to know him well and admire him. He would then take the boys and girls to two houses beside each other which he owned. Next day he got rid of the girls and chose amongst the boys which he would keep. It took a long time to find him out, but after a spirited fight on his own behalf he was found Guilty and sentenced to 12 years.

An Appalling Abortion

Mary was the only child of a Dublin surgeon and his wife. She was 23, was employed as a secretary and lived at home with her parents. She had a nice, steady boy-friend and though not formally engaged they hoped to marry. Unfortunately she became pregnant by another man after a drinks party.

At an early stage of her pregnancy she was introduced to a shady Agency in one of the Dublin suburbs, which masqueraded as a Travel Agency but whose profitable business was arranging 'Abortion Tours' to London, abortion being unlawful in Ireland.

She was told at the office that the fee was £900 – half payable, in cash, to the Dublin Agency in advance of travel and the other half, in cash, to the Abortion Clinic in London on arrival. She could just manage the money and taking a week off from her job without anybody suspecting she paid her money and was told to report at Dun Laoghaire Port wearing a red head-scarf. She would then be taken to London by car with three other girls. She told her unsuspecting parents that she was having a week off with a girl-friend and they were delighted.

At a place in London which she could not identify she paid the balance of the money to the 'Matron' and had the Abortion next day at the hands of a doctor she had never met before. Something went wrong with the abortion, because though it was successful she was left bleeding profusely and they could not stop it.

Although her return journey was booked they got a car and deposited her on a seat in Sloane Square, where she stretched out to overcome her weakness and pain.

A woman passing by soon saw her and immediately rushed her by taxi to a doctor friend. He managed to stifle the bleeding and put her in a Home nearby for the night. He examined her fully the next morning. Being convinced that the operation was an illegal one – by being outside the quota and not registered – he told her that there would be no charge for his examinations or the Home and insisted upon 'lending' her the fare back to Dublin. He recommended that she should see a solicitor and named his own.

That is how she came to me and told me the full story. I was particularly cross about the callous way they had disposed of her in Sloane Square.

I first suggested the question of prosecution, but there were two objections to that; she had no idea where the clinic was and secondly she did not want the matter publicised in the Irish papers.

I said that the police might help us to locate the clinic as they had a record of all licensed clinics. But, understandably, she would not change her mind on publicity.

What could one do to help her, and help others?

Taking Dublin first, I said I knew a Chief Superintendent of the Garda and I would write to him, if she agreed, telling him the facts of the case (suppressing her name) and ask him if he could arrange a close watch on the Agency. She was agreeable and I draft/wrote the letter then and there. I got back a letter saying that he would put the matter in hand immediately. A few months later my solicitor told me that they had been prosecuted – for Income Tax frauds! They were not able to account for cash payments. The fine (£20,000) soon closed them down.

So far as London was concerned I asked my solicitor if he would tell a senior police officer the facts – withholding the client's name – and ask him if he could find out the clinic's name and keep a watch on it. He was most co-operative and within a week gave him the clinic's name and address and said the police would make a few random raids, but they came to nothing – except that only two Irish girls were registered for the day in question.

It was all one could do to help. But I was delighted to hear from the solicitor later on that – nobody suspecting – she had married her original boyfriend.

Muloody's Memoirs

Horace Muloody, senior counsel in the Irish Bar was the undoubted leader of the Irish Pollution Bar. It all started soon after pupilage when he did and won a small case about dirty drains. From a solicitor, who witnessed his success he got his second brief on the subject, successfully defending a pig-farmer for polluting a river, by showing that it was an Ostrich farmer lower down who was responsible.

Bit by bit he got cases concerning poisoned air, fumes, smoke, factories, noise and the safety of seas, lakes and swimming pools. He wrote an immense tome called 'The Law of Pollution', which became one of the standard text-books on the subject.

Shortly before retirement he told his fellow Benchers at the King's Inns in Dublin that he had just completed his Memoirs, which ran to 628 pages in type-script. But he was puzzled about the title. Being at heart a simple man he rather favoured 'My Recollections of Pollution'.

Suggestions kept pouring in.

'Why not 'Stagnant Waters',' said one.

'Or 'Filthy Waters',' said another.

'Or 'Dirty Drains'.'

'Pure Air'.'

'Something crisper,' said a Junior Bencher, 'like 'Clearing The Air'.'

'Why not get away from Pollution,' said another and call it, say, 'Women I have known in Pollution'?'

'I never had any women clients,' said Muloody sadly. 'And anyway I'm happily married.

'You'd catch the women's market if you called it 'Women's Part in the Pollution Battle'.'

'It would mean further research and re-writing a lot of the book.'

'I'm all for bringing girls into it,' said one young Bencher. 'It sells. Why not 'Our Girls Are So Fresh And So Healthy'?'

'Or,' said someone else, 'Love In The Fresh Air'?'

Another said, 'Why not get away from girls and have something startling? As I know you once acted for the German Embassy before the War. Why not call it 'I was Hitler's counsel'?'

'Well I suppose I was in a sense. But it only lasted a day and a half and I was never paid for it.'

'Gives me an idea, ' said a senior bencher. 'Why not make it international. Something like 'Fog Over Europe'.'

'Why not call it simply 'Bird'?'

'Or 'Dirty Cases'?'

The young Bencher came back to girls again but they didn't sound right.

Muloody thanked them all and went off to think. He finally called the Memoirs 'An Unusual Barrister's Memoirs'.

One day about four months later Metro was talking to Goldwyn and Meyer: 'I suggest we buy this book. It's got a lot in it. Have a cursory read of it.'

They decided to pay Muloody thousands and they made a best-selling film out of it, having no relevance whatever to the book, except vaguely in the title – 'The Girl In The River'.

Baby Snatching

Mrs L was a woman of 31, respectable in every sense of the word but living apart from her husband, a shopkeeper. They had no family, which disappointed them both. Indeed it was probably the reason they parted. She had had three miscarriages.

It is a grave mistake for people to leave young babies alone in their prams outside supermarkets or shops. It ought in fact be made a criminal offence.

One Friday afternoon a mother left a one-and-a-half year old boy outside a supermarket. With the weekend coming she was rather longer than she expected. But the baby and pram had gone. She made enquiries of passers-by but they could not help. She then went to the police.

However it took the police four months to find the baby, in Mrs L's possession. She lived in a house of her own and only took the baby out at night. One night, rather late, two policemen on patrol saw a woman wheeling a pram with a baby in it. Being suspicious at the late hour for a baby they stopped Mrs L and questioned her. After a few stupid lies and amidst many tears she confessed that she had stolen the baby four months before outside the supermarket. She was arrested, and refused bail. The baby, none the worse for his experience, was restored to his mother.

I was briefed to defend. At the Magistrate's Court I applied for Bail but it was refused. Mrs L was returned for trial at the Old Bailey.

There was no possible defence so she had to plead Guilty.

I put forward as mitigation all the facts mentioned above, stressing that the baby had been looked after very well. Presumptuously perhaps, I asked the judge to consider a Conditional Discharge or Probation. 'She has already been in prison,' I said, 'for over two months.' The judge said, 'Mrs L you must go to prison for this wicked and heartless offence. You know it was wrong. You never thought of the parents' anguish for four whole months. It was a purely selfish thing to do. For all you cared the parents might have thought that the baby had been murdered. You will go to prison for six months, not counting the two months you have already spent.'

Under pressure from the solicitor and client we decided to appeal. I thought that the sentence would stand – indeed be thought inadequate.

Because of the relatively short period involved we had to apply for the appeal to be expedited, which it was.

The Lord Chief Justice, delivering the Judgment of the Court, echoed the trial judge's remarks and said, 'Moreover you have put the police to a great deal of trouble, searching for missing babies, suspecting possible murder of the baby and possible export of him abroad.'

Then he said, 'Bearing in mind that you have now experienced prison for the first time in your life and have learned a good lesson we propose to substitute a sentence which will release you six weeks from today.'

Frisky Phyllis

Rumour had it – that a well-known set of Chancery Chambers in Lincoln's Inn had a great liking for modest gambling. Horses, Pools, Draws – there was no Lotto in those days; no scratch cards. There were seven of them in Chambers and Higgleshank QC was the Head of Chambers.

It was because of him that they were about £500 up on the Horses, in their three years activity. He had two good Trainers as clients.

They had never had a word from Littlewoods or Vernons.

They entered for every draw they could find but nothing of any value turned up. Only an electric toaster, three bath towels, a weekend for two in Southend, a baby's cot and a pair of skates.

Then suddenly they won fifth prize in a draw – a greyhound called Frisky Phyllis, with one year's free training. It was a prize they had never dreamt of and Higgleshank QC was very worried about the name. 'Nothing of this must leak out,' he said, 'and we must run it under a special syndicate name.'

They all went to Harringay to see the animal and its affable trainer Patsy Murphy. She looked thin, unhappy and lifeless. 'Don't worry about that,' said Mr Murphy, 'I've only just taken her over from a half-baked trainer from Limerick. I'll soon put bounce back into her again.'

'What sort of form has she?', asked the Junior member of Chambers.

'Third at Clonmel before she came over here. The change of air may do her good.'

'When does she first race?'

'I thought of trying her out on Thursday week but don't expect

40

much. A couple of quid for a place.

'Be sure,' said Higgleshank, 'to race her under the ownership of Trust Deed.'

'Right oh,' replied the trainer leading her away.

On Thursday week all attended the evening meeting. They all agreed that she had gone off, if that was possible.

She came in fifth. 'A good start,' said optimistic Mr Murphy.

'We must sell her,' said Higgleshank on the way home.

'Who'd buy her?', enquired a member of Chambers.

'Give her to the Trainer,' suggested another.

'Doubt if he'd take her,' commented a colleague.

Next day the Head of Chambers was pestered with telephone calls from Mr Murphy. 'Old Frisky seems to have caught a chill. The new air doesn't seem to suit her at all. I'll keep you posted.'

'I think it's pneumonia. Better send for the Vet – again.'

'Vet says touch and go.'

'Could you give me your weekend number in case anything happens.'

Twice during the week-end Mr Murphy was on the telephone.

'I don't suppose we could come to some sort of arrangement under the new plea-bargaining system?'

'She's battling on but I don't like the croak in her throat.' On the Sunday, 'The croak's gone but she's sweating horrible. I've got the vet again.'

'Vet's worried by her but maybe it might pass.'

On Monday all were in Court and it was the – intention to give them a full medical history of Frisky Phyllis. But a dejected clerk met him and said, 'Very brief message, sir 'Regret Frisky Phyllis deceased'.'

After a short interval they resumed gambling – but on horses only.

Cooney's Contempt

A story of my father's from the old Munster Circuit – There was a newly-appointed, very self-satisfied judge, dressed in sparkling red new robes, sitting on Assizes for the first time. He was trying a case about the ownership of a four acre island in the middle of a lough (or lake). It was a cold and wintry day at the beginning of December and there seemed no point at all in his visiting the island, but on the morning of the second day he said that he intended to and wanted all counsel, solicitors and staff to be present, robed.

Cabs were laid on and this impressive procession moved on to the lough, about 15 miles away.

At the end of one of the party's land the judge asked, 'Where are the boats?' One of the barristers said timorously, 'But Your Lordship is not going to visit the actual island, are you?', to be met with the reply, 'Of course I am, and so are you all.'

The parties knew where the local boat-men lived. There were only three of them, so it would need at least double-trips.

The boat-men came and the first load was naturally the judge and his Clerk. They crossed safely to the island through choppy waters. But as the Clerk was escorting His Lordship on to the island he fell in. In loud and irritated tones the judge said, 'Get my clerk somebody.'

The clerk was rolling about and shouting, when one of the solicitors leapt in and pulled him back to shore. The judge eyed his clerk up and down and said, 'That was a very stupid thing to do, Hodge.'

Hodge unaccountably said, 'My apologies, My Lord. I am terribly sorry.'

The judge then said, 'Take these two away and have them dried out. 'Turning to the Registrar he said, 'You will act as my Clerk until Hodge recovers.'

It was icily cold and heavy rain began to fall. 'Get me my umbrella, Mr Registrar, it's in my boat.' The Registrar ran and got it before the new robes were damaged.

As everybody looked around this desolate island they saw nothing but sheep – dozens and dozens of sheep.

'Are they yours?', the judge asked each party. Both said No, they didn't keep sheep. 'Whose are they?'

The parties were reluctant to disclose. One said to his counsel, 'He's a rough, tough, ould divil.'

But eventually his name was disclosed – Patsy Cooney, who farmed land between the two claimants.

'Have Cooney before me at two o'clock, Mr Registrar.'

'I think I'll need police assistance, My Lord.'

'I'll get it,' said the judge. 'How far is the nearest town?'

'Three miles aback the way you've cum,' said one of the boat-men. They left the island, safely. In driving back they stopped at the police station and a startled serjeant said that he – and a couple of officers – would have Cooney before His Lordship at two o'clock. 'But shouldn't he have a piece of paper?'

The judge obliged and put a lot of threats into the document.

At two o'clock Cooney, with an escort of three policemen appeared before His Lordship. He was a mixture of truculence and surprise.

'Are you Cooney?' The judge did not believe in it.

'Yes, an' watcher want me for?'

'Whose sheep are on that island near you?'

'Moin.

'How long have they been there?'

'Abou tree munths.'

'Did you know about this case?'

'Evryun did.'

'Why did you put your sheep there?'

'Place going to waste. Good grass.'

'Have you any claim to this land?'

'Nun at all. Let 'em fight it out between themselves.'

'I'm going to commit you for Contempt of Court until further order.'

'What does that mean?'

'Jail. And be sure you get the sheep away as soon as possible.'

'How can I? I have no-one to help me.'

'You got them there. Now get them back the same way. Take him down, officers.' The judge went on with the case and reserved Judgment to Dublin next term. On the last day of the Assizes Patsy Cooney, represented by solicitor and counsel, applied for his release to the same judge. The proceedings lasted two minutes. 'Are the sheep still there?', enquired His Lordship.

'Yes . . . but . . . ,' began his counsel.

'Application dismissed.'

At the beginning of the New Year he applied to the vacation judge in Dublin. 'No,' said the judge. 'The sheep are still there and I take as serious a view of that as my learned brother.'

Just before term started they applied again to the vacation judge, now their original judge. 'Ah,' said the judge. 'Cooney the sheep trespasser. Are the sheep still on the island?'

'Yes, My Lord, but . . .'

The judge was about to say 'Application Dismissed' when counsel said, 'But there has been a happy ending. The parties in the suit became worried about the court costs, so the day before yesterday they completed a sale of the island to Mr Cooney. So, My Lord, he has his own sheep on his own land.'

Complimentary

When I was a young barrister I was scared stiff of leading counsel, particularly Chancery ones, who seemed so solemn as to be weighed down with their own knowledge.

I was lucky enough to get my biggest brief up to then, to be led by Ungoed Thomas KC of the Chancery Bar for the Chief Constables of England and Wales on a pay claim arbitration. Before getting the Brief my knowledge of them was so slight that I believed it was a purely honourary office.

Our preliminary Consultation was at 4.30 p.m. in my Leader's Chambers in Lincoln's Inn. A good 10 minutes early I was ushered into the Waiting Room by his Clerk – a Waiting Room already filled by menacing-looking Chief Constables, some in heavily silver-buttoned, well ribboned uniforms, others in dark and expensive suiting.

They looked at me with slight puzzlement when I came in. I clearly wasn't a Chief Constable. What was I? Seeing me with a bundle of papers they probably thought I was their KC's office boy.

At that moment our Instructing solicitor arrived and with a wave at them greeted me. Their sense of mystery deepened.

The Clerk came in, and my stock rose when he said, 'Mr Comyn, Mr Ungoed Thomas would like to see you alone for a short while before the Consultation. He wants to discuss some points of law with you.'

Ungoed Thomas and I had never met before and we introduced each other. He asked me affectionately about Holroyd Pearce, my Landlord and Ex-Master. He asked me who else was in Chambers with me. He asked me about myself.

Then we had a few words about the case. 'It'll really run itself,' he said. 'Marginal increases all round I should think.' Then he added, naming the two smaller counties, 'I feel that Rutland and Huntingdon ought to get more.' I agreed.

'Being serious,' he said 'would you like to deal with them? The Arbitrators will be tired of my voice by then.'

I said yes of course. 'And when I have digested the Brief fully,' he said, 'there may be other counties for you to deal with.'

I liked the word 'digested' and kept it for further use. I had of course digested and redigested every word of my Brief.

The clients (plus a great many chairs) were brought in. They now eyed me with considerable awe. Having been called in first, 'to discuss some points of law' I was obviously the lawman of the partnership. This was reinforced when the Leader began by saying,

'Comyn, thank you for those few words. They have cheered my mind considerably.'

We then sat down to a long and patient consultation. But the leader's courtesy did not end there. Every so often he used to turn to me and say, 'That's your point, isn't it, Comyn' or 'We're agreed on that, Comyn?'

The Chief Constables left after about two-and-a-half hours, satisfied that they had an excellent KC and a rather good Junior. I left with the firm feeling that if I ever took Silk I would be as courteous and kind as this Leader was to me. The case came on for hearing and was settled at the Court door, with our now smiling Chief Constables getting a good rise in pay.

Concealment of Death

A solicitor from the West of England rang up at about 5 p.m. and asked to me see me in consultation tomorrow without fail.

Clement, my splendid Clerk, came into my room, told me about it and said we were full up all tomorrow, even at lunch-time (when Masters took short summonses). We knew him; he was of a highly respectable firm from Cornwall, named Crimshaw. He'd been to see me three or four times before. How could we manage it, Clem asked. He'd suggested my staying on late in the evening but the solicitor said he would have to get back that night. Clem said that he would ring him back after he had a word with me.

'Did he tell you what the case was about?'

'I naturally asked him,' said Clem, but very apologetically he said he simply could not help me on this occasion.

We thought for a moment. 'Look,' I said, 'tell him I can see him at home tonight at any time he comes. Or otherwise after his overnight train gets in early tomorrow morning. Tell him too that if necessary I'll give him a bed tonight and see that he gets the first train back in the morning. And tell him exactly where I live. Clement came back in five minutes. 'He's most grateful. He'll come up tonight. There's a train in an hour and a half's time. He's very thankful about the bed.'

At about a quarter to one Mr. Grimshaw arrived. Having refreshed him he said, 'Very good of you to see me at this ungodly hour but as you'll see it's very urgent. The police are about to start ripping up my client's home and digging up his garden.'

He then proceeded to tell me the story. His client was a very large landowner. He and his wife had two boys working abroad, and a daughter, aged 24, who was the apple of their eye. She died of peritonitis a week ago.

'They're not Christian Scientists,' he said, 'but belong to some sect which won't have doctors. So did she, otherwise the poor little thing wouldn't have died.'

'Before I go on,' he said, 'I'm worried as to whether I should tell the police – or indeed you – about a crime which I know has been committed.'

'No,' I said, 'you're absolutely privileged – completely privileged to keep your client's instructions. So am 1. What you're thinking about is counselling a crime about to be committed.'

'Thank God for that. Well, he and his wife can't bear to be parted from her so a few nights ago they buried her in a large wood they have near the house, and then they pretended that she had disappeared suddenly.'

'They didn't cremate her,' I asked, 'and bury the ashes?'

'No,' he said, 'better if they had, but this religion doesn't believe in it. They just put her in a large box. As her mother pathetically told me they wanted to be able to visit her every day.'

'Every day would be liable to leave marks,' I commented.

'I've seen the grave,' he answered. 'Very well concealed and covered all round with thick gorse wood.'

'But surely, Mr. Grimshaw, they have servants who'd know the girl was ill, indeed dead, and that she just didn't disappear?'

'They have four long-standing servants but all of the same sect. They would say nothing at all about the illness, the absence of a doctor or even about the death.'

'How did the police get to know about it?'

'Before he came to me, you'd hardly believe it, he went to them and reported her missing.'

'Presumably knowing about him and his odd views.'

'They're not thinking of murder but what they're really

thinking of is concealment of death, evasion of inquest and illegal burial.'

'I had a word with the Inspector and he said that our options are open until they find the body.'

'Do you think they're likely to find it?'

'Not in the conventional places like the house or the garden but they could with sniffer dogs.'

'Well,' I said, 'the choices are doing nothing, hoping they won't find anything or else confessing all.'

'Confessing all,' he said, 'the clients simply wouldn't.'

'Why?, It's not selling the clients up the river, Mr. Grimshaw. If the police don't find anything now they'll go on and on literally for ever. With this over your clients' heads all the time.'

'I see that,' he said slowly, 'but I'm pretty sure the clients won't.' 'I know they'd agree to an inquest and they'd be tried but I feel very confident we'd get them off fairly lightly. And maybe we could fix up a good place in a local cemetery where they could visit her as often as they wished. But of course it's up to them.'

'Could you see them, Mr. Comyn? Or – I hesitate to ask it – but could you come down to see them, perhaps this weekend? They're not very anxious to move with all these police around.'

'Alright. I'll come down this weekend – Saturday to Sunday evening. Take me to see them and where they have the grave.'

'Very good of you,' he said, adding with a smile, 'I'll give you a bed that night. We'll fix up the times of the trains later.'

We then had a very late night supper and he went to bed, but 1 had him up bright and early for his train.

We met on the Saturday and he drove me out to see the clients' house and immediate grounds, still with police, probing and digging; and there were sniffer dogs with police escorts. No chance of seeing the grave until nightfall.

They were a very charming couple in their mid–fifties but so deeply involved religiously and emotively that it was difficult to make them see what we thought was sense. The solicitor had come thoroughly round to my point of view.

We talked and talked for over four hours. No good. Then when the police had withdrawn and when it was dusk the solicitor and I went to see the grave. It was well hidden and completely covered and surrounded by twigs, fallen leaves and brambles. It was hard to believe that there was a grave there.

Next morning we met the clients again. The owner said, 'I've had a long talk with my wife. She's more disposed to take your advice, Mr. Comyn, than I am. She's very worried. Well, so am I for that matter, but I try not to show it. Could we have another talk, all four of us?'

We talked for the rest of the morning. His wife said she could not bear the thought of the police hanging round and everybody finding the grave. He said he had no fear of them discovering anything, but the police attention was upsetting.

I said, 'It's entirely a matter for both of you, And whatever you decide we'll stand right behind you all the way.'

They asked me exactly what would happen if they confessed. I said that Mr. Crimshaw will have a first-rate pathologist ready to confirm the cause of death, there would have to be an Inquest but they need not trouble about that and there would have to be a trial but I felt fairly confident about that.

'Where would our daughter be buried?,' he asked.

Mr. Crimshaw said he thought he could arrange it for a nearby cemetery in some quiet place, readily accessible to them.

'We'll give you our decision before lunch.'

Just before lunch they came back. 'We have decided – reluctantly – to take your advice. When do we do it?'

'Tomorrow or Tuesday,' I suggested, 'in order to give Mr. Crimshaw a chance to lay on a pathologist and see what he can do about a cemetery.'

'Is there any chance of leaving my wife out of it?' he asked.

'I'm afraid not. But I'm sure he will see how the police react. Meanwhile he and I will retire for half an hour to draft a short statement for your both to hand to the police and Coroner's Officer. And be sure to say nothing else.' It actually took us over an hour to draft the statement.

It was Tuesday afternoon before they went to the police. They were accompanied by Mr. Grimshaw and were well received. They were both charged and given police bail. Mr. Grimshaw reported to me at once.

It took two days to get the Exhumation Order. The Home

Office soon readily agreed that the death was due to peritonitis.

I attended the inquest which passed off without comment – a mild observation by the coroner that it seemed to him a pity and sad that the deceased girl and her parents held such views about medicine but that of course was their affair. The verdict was 'Natural Causes'.

The girl was interred in a charming plot kindly donated by some local family in their small private cemetery.

Two months later the case came up at the local Assizes. Two charges – concealment of death and unlawful burial, with of course, pleas of Guilty. The judge was a kind and understanding man. He too obviously read the papers – including our statement – before Court. He listened in silence to the Crown's opening speech which was factual and not unsympathetic.

He listened to my first few sentences of instructions and then interrupted me. 'Mr. Comyn, people simply must not act in this illegal fashion. It gives everybody a lot of trouble and worries them as to whether there has been foul play. But that said, it is understandable in this case and was done indeed with the kindest and saddest of motives. I am quite sure that people in general need no lesson about this sort of thin which is happily very rare. I'm sure your clients kind and helpful people, will never offend again. There's nothing at all to be gained by punishing them any more. I propose to give them an Absolute Discharge'.

The Back

When the case was called, the judge said to counsel, 'Gentlemen, I see this case is about an injured back – an alleged injured back. I feel I ought to tell you that I myself have an injured back – though few know it, and it would, of course, make no difference at all about my trying this case. I injured it, as a matter of fact, in the Grand National – but that is, of course, a long time ago now. Would you, gentlemen, have a word with your solicitors about my taking this case?'

Meanwhile, the judge's clerk was tucking in a large red cushion behind His Lordship's back, accompanied by little twinges of pain from the latter.

Counsel for the claimant did not bother to take instructions at all. 'No objection at all, m'Lord'. His opposite number, acting for the insurers, turned to their solicitors and murmured, 'What bloody awful luck, but I suppose we'd better go on with him. No one knows who we'd get instead'. The insurers reluctantly agreed; after all, this was according to them, a 'sham' injury and this judge ought to be able to sort that one out as well as any other. So their counsel said he agreed.

The judge then said, 'Well, I've been wondering these last few minutes if I ought to agree. Not, as I think I've said, it would make any difference to me – one way or the other. But one must think of the parties. In this case – indeed, in any case – one party must win and the other lose; one wants no feeling of discrimination'.

Counsel for the claimant, anxious not to lose his tribunal, wagged his wigged head vigorously. Its opposite number felt that a neutral track was advisable – 'Whatever Your Lordship feels'.

'Well', said the judge, 'you have both agreed and why should I stand in the way? If I wasn't trying this case, I'd be trying another, perhaps involving injuries. Let us commence'!

After the claimant's counsel had opened the case, he called his client, a bent-over, shuffling, half-staggering man in his forties. He spoke into his chest, which caused constant interruption from the shorthand writer, who said that she could not hear. 'Move over closer to him', repeated the judge until eventually she, too, was crouching down beside him.

'I can hear him perfectly well', said the judge proudly, 'but then I'm facing him and not bent down over a book. Which doesn't mean, incidentally, that I take no notice. Can everyone else hear him?'

'Yes', they said.

The claimant told of the accident which threw him off a high lorry from which he was throwing pitch. When cross-examined, he denied that he had fallen on grass and insisted that it was the road. He naturally denied being a sham.

He was a widower, who lived alone, and he found a little

awkwardness in questions about dressing himself and tying his shoes, until the judge interrupted by saying, 'With some back conditions, it is strangely easier to do these things. But I'm not, of course, saying that that case is this case'.

He called two neighbours to support his condition and they were naturally cross-examined as to why they were not two other neighbours.

He had two doctor witnesses, with degrees, and appointments which filled two pages of the shorthand book. Professor Brown had written a standard text book on The Lower Back and his colleague, Mr. Alistair Godwin, had produced a book on *The Back Generally*. In this respect, they were one up on the opposition, who could only cross-examine from Mr. Graham Cadwallader's *Neck to Spine*.

The claimant's two doctors vouched for the genuineness of his injuries. 'Typical of the type of injuries he suffered', said Professor Brown. 'A pain injury to the whole bark region', echoed Mr. Godwin, 'amply illustrated at pages 297 and 298 of my book on *The Back Generally*'.

'My client admits inciting violence, injuring the police and throwing smoke-bombs, m'lud, but would like to congratulate you on your recent brave stand against prison sentences . . .'

The insurers had two doctors, whom it transpired they always used, and who had never given evidence for a claimant in their lives. Mr. Cadwallader of Neck to Spine – said the injuries were all sham. 'A black eye you can see', he said, 'but the inside of a back you cannot see; so an injured back is the easiest to fake'.

Horace Horsfall, F.R.C.S. etc., agreed, 'You can usually tell by a man's reaction how he really feels. Especially by contrasting reactions on different occasions'.

Mr. Horsfall won approval from the judge by saying, incidentally, that he knew 'and had a very high respect for' the judge's own orthopaedic surgeon.

After speeches by counsel came the moment – or rather many moments – of judgment.

The claimant had won. £40,000 damages and costs.

The insurance manager was furious and went up to the claimant in the court corridor. 'If it takes every penny we have, I'll have you watched for the rest of your life'.

The claimant eyed him (with upturned eyes) and said, 'I'm off to Lourdes tomorrow'.

'Why didn't you go yesterday?'

'I didn't have the money'.

Boozled

It was a great pity that the personal injuries case was listed 'Not before two o'clock' and that it looked as if it was going to come on precisely at two o'clock. A greater pity still that it was before a charming and courteous High Court judge, who was – however – a strict teetotaller.

My plaintiff, whom I liked very much, took our advice to reject the £8,000 paid into Court and to aim for £12,000 plus. He had been knocked down when crossing the street; the defence was that he 'dashed out', giving the motorist no chance. One of his great merits was that he did not put the case of his injuries too high.

The trouble was that the plaintiff and his eye-witness returned at 1.45 p.m. from lunch completely shimozzled. Their laughter and ribaldry could be heard in the Central Hall downstairs. The plaintiff tried an Irish jig; the eye-witness a Highland fling. They fell over and my junior had to help them up.

Despondently I said to our instructing solicitor 'We'd better take the money in Court. Lock them in a Lavatory while I negotiate. We don't want the other side to see them'.

He said 'Trouble about that is how do we get our boozie client to agree properly?'

I saw the force of that.

'Alright', I said, 'Lock them in the Lavatory anyway and I'll try to negotiate again. It'll keep the judge waiting, which is a good thing. And above all get our two doctors here as quick as light'.

'But we've arranged tomorrow morning for them. They'll be furious'.

'Tell them it's very, very urgent – but for God's sake don't say why'.

After twenty minutes of negotiating, my opponent would only come up with another £500 and costs.

So we had to go into Court.

I opened at some length. Then, seeing one of the doctors arriving, I said 'I will call the two doctors first'.

'That's a little unusual, Mr. Comyn. We usually have the plaintiff first'.

'It's an unusual case, My Lord, in many ways'.

'Ah well, if you say so. After all, Mr. Comyn, it's up to you to decide who you'll call and when'.

My opponent got up, 'I haven't got my doctors here. We requested them for tomorrow morning, in anticipation that the case will take its usual course'.

I nipped in quickly, 'My learned friend has seen our medical reports and I expect that my doctors will give evidence in accordance with them. If any point arises I can have them back tomorrow'.

An already irate doctor became visibly irater.

It was just a quarter to four when he had finished his evidence. The other even irater doctor had arrived.

I had to get him up to about five o'clock because this judge sat late and anyway would want to let the doctor away.

At five to five this doctor finished. I had just made it – on hand. The learned judge said 'Mr. Comyn, shall we just swear in the Plaintiff and get a few details of him, name, address, age, occupation?'

I had to think quickly. 'Might we leave that to the morning? I will want to speak to him, others may want to speak to him, and we couldn't do so if he was under oath'.

'Yes', said the judge, 'I'd forgotten that. You're quite right. I'll rise now'.

We unlocked a slightly sober plaintiff and eye-witness from the lavatory, where both had gone to sleep.

'Now look here you two', I said, 'I'm going to get you in a Temperance House for the night'.

Both pleaded splitting headaches and abdominal sickness and, on their solemn undertaking to take nothing alcoholic, we let them go.

Next morning all was well. When the plaintiff had finished his evidence the judge said to me, 'You were quite right to invite the doctors first. It has helped me enormously'.

The plaintiff got £12,500 and costs.

Indecency

On coming out of the underground at a South London Station, I went to the Gentleman's. A voice beside me suddenly spoke, 'You were lucky this morning, Mr. Comyn. We get over ten per cent of the indecencies here'.

I recognised him immediately as one of the two police officers I had cross-examined that morning at Bow Street when I successfully defended a 50-year old from Grosvenor Gardens on a charge of gross indecency at that very same place.

We chatted for about ten minutes. I pointed out to him – as I had to the Court – that their great weakness was not having got the other man. 'He slipped us', he said. I replied, 'What – with two of you there?' 'It sometimes happens', he said – but not very convincingly to me.

'Do you ever make mistakes?'

'Rarely', he replied.

'This seems a pretty awful job, yours'.

'You get used to it', he said.

'How often do you do it?'

'Five nights a week, except for time off – and spells of other duty'.

'Do you get many cases?'

'Hundreds', he said, 'This is probably the warmest spot in London'.

'Do they all go to Bow Street?' I did not like one court having the monopoly of these men's evidence.

'Yes', he said, 'mostly;.

'Do you suspect people in advance or just act when you see something?'

'Both', he said.

The other officer was hovering in the vestibule, ostensibly reading an evening paper. We nodded at each other and I went on my way. 'Good night, sir, happy hunting'.

'That would surely be apter for you', I replied.

I was dreadfully shocked to read in the paper a few days later that my client had committed suicide, shooting himself in his master's garden.

Fired

> I was an Usher
> But I got fired,
> For asking three cheers
> When my judge retired

Affidavit Annie

I am Affidavit Annie,
I have sworn 88,
I'm the matron of a girl's school
Where the parents litigate.

I am called upon when parents
Go to law with one another,
And it really is a battle
When a father fights a mother.

All the fashionable parents
Of distinction and of breeding
Start competing for my favours
When they're custody proceeding.

All the odds are in their favour
When my Affidavit's filed,
For the judges know my views
Are in the interests of the child.

I am Affidavit Annie
All there's now produced and shown
An Affidavit Album
Of the people I have known.

Divorce of course is now beyond
The slightest criticism
And the girls are better versed in it
Than in their Catechism.

We have to cater for it now
Whatever we may feel,
For the practice is so prevalent
Amongst our clientele.

I've had twenty seven Ladies
And at least a couple of Earls,
And innumerable Barons
Who were interested in girls.

I have also had a Viscount
And a Duke and Marchioness,
And I'm glad to say that each of them
Provided a success.

I've been swearing Affidavits now
For nigh on thirty years,
And I'm very highly thought of
In the realms of the peers.

I have sworn affidavits
For the high-ups in the Forces,
And could tell you quite a lot about
The facts of their divorces.

I've got brisk and breezy Admirals
Well out of troubled waters
And have won for them the custody
Of admirable daughters.

I've had Brigadiers and Colonels
Who got married late in life
And who fought their grimmest battles
Joining issue with the wife.

I have also had my moments
For the Diplomatic Corps,
I've had two or three Ambassadors
And Secretaries galore.

(These Diplomats I've noticed
Have a very marked addiction
For bringing girls for holidays
Beyond the Jurisdiction).

I've been also very active
For the members of the stage,
In the years when getting custody
Was reckoned all the rage.

I well remember one of them,
Who lived for years at Claridges,
And sought my helpful services
In three successive marriages.

Another I remember
Was well known upon the screen,
And summonses for custody
Were part of her routine.

She retained a leading counsel,
Though I never saw the need,
For throughout the whole proceedings
She would always play the lead.

She seemed to take her summonses
Incredibly to heart,
But I think the explanation was
She rather liked the part.

I have acted for a soccer star
A trainer and a jockey,
And the latter's youngest daughter
Stayed to captain us at hockey.

She serves as an example
Of a very special rule
That whoever I'm in favour of
I'm always for the School.

And I've acted for an Old Girl
Whom I once took oath about –
That there's something in heredity
I have not the slightest doubt.

Her mother and her father
Fought about her for a year,
And she fought about her children
Till she got them sent to here.

Yes, I'm Affidavit Annie
And I verify believe
That the school would miss me greatly
If I ever chanced to leave.

I have clients very satisfied
In Harley Street and Harrow,
In Bournemouth and Cheltenham
And even one in Barrow.

(I believe he was a Butcher,
He was certainly in trade,
But I don't care how he made himself
As long as he was made).

In every English County
I have parents who were patrons,
And they very kindly say that I'm
The paragon of matrons.

I am Affidavit Annie,
And I've not been wed myself
There are many compensations
For being left upon the shelf.

The King (Personally) v. Mylius

(R. v. Mylius, The Lord Chief Justice Alverstone and a Jury (1911))

Even before his betrothal to Princess May of Teck in 1893, there were rumours that the future King George V was already secretly married to someone else, who was still alive, and had borne him three children.

The rumours lingered intermittently but he tended to treat them with some amusement. It is, after all, a fairly common feature in history to find prominent people falsely accused of bigamy, or the father or mother of an illegitimate child.

In May 1910, he became King and the rumours revived in full force, emphasised by articles in a republican paper, the *Liberator*, published in Paris by a man called E.E. Mylius, and circulated from there to all British NWs. It asserted that the King had contracted a lawful marriage in 1890 in Malta with a daughter of Admiral Sir Michael Colme-Taylor and that there had been children.

The King was concerned about those articles, particularly the extent of their publication. He was advised in writing by his Law Officers (Sir Rufus Isaacs, K.C., and Sir John Simon, K.C.) who advised a prosecution. Mylius was arrested on December 26.

Constitutionally, the King – as the Fount of Justice – cannot give evidence. Nevertheless, Mylius, acting in person throughout, applied in Chambers to Lord Alverstone for the King to be subpoenaed. His application was duly refused.

In February 1911, Mylius, pleading Not Guilty to criminal libel, was tried by Lord Alverstone and a jury.

Admiral Sir Michael Culme-Taylor gave evidence that he assumed command of the Mediterranean Fleet at Malta in 1893 and was joined there by his wife and two daughters, who had never before been there.

He said that his younger daughter died unmarried in 1895, without having ever met the future King; his elder daughter Mary had not met him between 1879 – when she was eight – until 1895. She did not marry him at any time, much less when she was 19;

61

she in fact married the future Vice-Admiral Sir Trevelyan Napier in 1899.

Adding considerable strength to the case, Mary and her three brothers gave supporting evidence. It was also proved that the future King was not in Malta between 1888 and 1891, and that there was no record in the island registers of any marriage by him.

Mylius did not contradict any of this evidence, but again submitted strongly that the King be called as a witness. This was again refused on the ground that it was unconstitutional. The jury found Mylius Guilty and the Lord Chief Justice gave him the maximum sentence for the one libel alleged.

The Attorney General then read a statement by the King that he had only been married to the Queen and would have given such evidence in person had he not been advised by the Law Officers that it was unconstitutional for the Sovereign to go into the witness box.

There was great public sympathy with the King, the rumours at last died down but on Mylius's release, he returned to the attack in a pamphlet published in New York called 'The Morganatic Marriage of George V'.

Coup de Grace

I had two very pretty French girls to defend for having tendered a false fare on British Railways. They were not quite 21 and were au pairs at Winchester. They had two days off every fortnight and (as they told me in a mixed-language consultation) they decided to spend the night at Woking and go on to London next day. They could remember the name of the B and B but puetretre could find it again. I asked my instructing solicitor to go to Woking with them and find the place at all costs.

The father of one of them had come over from France to be with his daughter and kept saying that it was 'impossible'. The other had not told her parents.

Next morning – they said – they went to Woking Station, their train was in, they were in a hurry, they could not find a collector in his box, so they boarded the train, intending to pay at Waterloo, the terminal, the fare from Woking. To their surprise they were immediately arrested. They denied throughout that they had come from Winchester. Unfortunately our enquiries of their mistresses was of no help. One said she could not remember and the other refused to be 'mixed up in the case'.

On the morning of the hearing the solicitor told me that he had tramped Woking and suburbs with the girls but they could not find the B and B.

We pleaded Not Guilty.

The prosecution then called two witnesses to say that the Waterloo side of Woking Station was closed all that morning for repairs, and then the collector at Waterloo to say that he had been informed of that 'in the course of his duty'.

I asked the stipendiary magistrate if I might have a few minutes' adjournment.

'I thought you might,' he said stiffly. 'Tell me when you're ready.'

We went with the girls to the outside corridor, where in a deluge of tears, they confessed all.

The father kept saying what bad luck it was to have chosen that station and what a lovely girl his daughter was. They both said they had very little money, but father said, 'I have enough for both.'

We went back into Court and changed our plea to Guilty. The officer in charge of the case said there was nothing against either girl.

I mitigated as best I could. Towards the end the magistrate, a rough and tough character, said, 'Have they admitted their Guilt to you, Mr Comyn?'

Rightly or wrongly I was not prepared to answer that question and simply said, 'They have pleaded Guilty.'

An interpreter was produced. The magistrate pronounced sentence. 'You two foreign girls came over here and stole. You would have gone into the witness-box and committed perjury if you could. You are no advertisement for France. You are just nasty, wicked cheats. I don't expect you have much money – so I sentence each of you to seven days' imprisonment and a £30 fine

to be paid within those seven days, or six months imprisonment.'
He awarded no costs.

The girls were led away sobbing and we discussed the matter
in the corridor. It was a clever sentence, both as to the short term
of imprisonment and the low fine.

We would apply to a judge in chambers that afternoon or
tomorrow morning for Leave to Appeal and bail pending appeal.

We did so but after a long and careful hearing he dismissed
our application. 'In spite of their good record,' he said, 'I believe
this was the right sentence. It was not a spontaneous fraud but a
well thought out one. Persisted in to the very end and ready to be
supported by perjury. I believe that the short, sharp, shock of
imprisonment will bring these young women to their senses.'

Unless My Eyes Deceive Me

Seeing is not believing,
As any judge can say,
The witness who's deceiving
Will give himself away.

I've been around Assizes
For close on forty years,
I've heard so many lieses
I can't believe my ears.

They think that they deceive me
Who tell so many lies,
I'm sure that you'll believe me
But I can't believe my eyes.

The Song of the Bankrupt

O I hear a little whisper
About fudgery and fraud,
But preserve a little caution –
Don't go noising it abroad.

For if you should continue
You may find that you defame,
You are speaking rather lightly
Of what's in a lady's name.

Difference

Those with libelled reputation
Get enormous compensation,
More than for a leg or arm
Who sustained the greater harm?

Just

Just for a handful of silver he left us,
Eleventh the hour for returning his Brief,
Of valuable services thus he bereft us
Causing us chaos surpassing belief.

Twenty years now since that handful of silver,
Instructing solicitors think of it yet,
They've never sent him a Brief (for returning) –
Instructing solicitors never forget.

Richard Piggott (1829–1889)

Richard Piggott was an Irish journalist and from being an errand boy with The Nation became proprietor of The Irishman. His reputation was poor when he came to do battle with Charles Stewart Parnell (1846–1891) in the year before his death, in The Parnell Commission.

Parnell, leader of the Irish Party in the House of Commons, was notably a pacific man, although organisations which he supported – such as The Land League – on occasions resorted to violence. Parnell condemned violence and preferred Parliamentary means to further his republicanism.

In 1882, there occurred 'The Phoenix Park Murders'. Parnell expressed in the House of Commons his detestation of the murders. Yet five years later, *The Times* published articles under the title 'Parnellism and Crime' publishing a facsimile of a letter, in Parnell's handwriting, it was said, warmly welcoming 'The Phoenix Park Murders' very soon after them. Some claimed to recognise Parnell's writing; a recognised handwriting expert swore that it was. Parnell simply denied it in the House of Commons, when a Special Commission under three judges was appointed to inquire into The Times allegations. Parnell wanted his countryman, Charles Russell, QC, to appear for him and so much did the latter want to do so, that after six month's argument, he broke his retainer to act for *The Times*.

At the Commission in 1889, the first question was from whom *The Times* obtained the letter and it was said that it was from an anti-Parnellite named Houston who had obtained it from Richard Piggott. When the latter was called, he said that he had got it from a Parnellite in return for a bribe. In the letter the word 'hesitancy' had been spelt 'hesitency'. In a careful cross-examination designed to put Piggott off, and guard him against corrections, Charles Russell asked him eventually to write down some words. He then solemnly and carefully, gave him a list of words which appeared to have nothing to do with the case, and then – as an apparent afterthought – 'leaving spaces write the word 'hesitancy' – with a small 'h''. Piggott wrote the word as 'hesitency'. Piggott was betrayed as a forger and a perdurer, which he finally admitted.

Counsel for *The Times* withdrew and the newspaper settled Parnell's claim for £5,000.

The other part of the Commission found that Parnell had failed to denounce agrarian violence. It was a weak and odd finding after a hearing of 128 days; Parnell had been supported by Little, but his amendment to delete it was defeated. Piggott absconded and was found to have committed suicide in Madrid.

At this time, Parnell had been long associating with Mrs. Kitty O'Shea, and her husband cited them both in undefended divorce proceedings. This caused a scandal in both Ireland and England. On June 28, 1891 Parnell married Mrs O'Shea but he only lived for five months after and died aged 44. He is buried in Glasnevin Cemetery, Dublin.

When Judges make Mistakes

Even judges can make mistakes! On fact and law! When they do, it is costly – to the losing litigant in the Court of Appeal. For such an event my argument is that the costs of both sides – 'here and below' should normally be borne out of state funds; a special fund kept for that purpose. Because it is the fault of Her Majesty's judge, the State judge. Take for example a complex case on fact and law which lasts 20 working days, one month. On fact, there are many judicial errors possible; on law, a multitude more. The learned judge may find there is no authority, and go wrong in making one. Or he may go wrong in choosing between two conflicting authorities. Or he may misinterpret a case. Or else follow a different line of case, which proves to be wrong.

In some cases he may be misled by argument on one side or the other (they should not get their costs); but in many cases the fault will lie with him – creation of new law, the wrong preference between two conflicting cases, then mis-interpretation of a case or cases.

In the famous *Thetis* case, arising out of the tragic loss of the submarine in Liverpool Bay just before war broke out in 1939, all three Courts dealing with the matter took diametrically opposing views on fact and law – *Duncan and Craven v. Cammell Laird and Others* [1946] A.C. 40; the trial judge (Mr. Justice Wrottesley) found Cammell Laird to blame. The Court of Appeal found only Lt. Woods, the submarine officer, to blame. The House of Lords found nobody to blame. And the widows (fortunately supported by a union) were condemned in all the costs. Why?

And this still goes on in other cases.

I do not suggest an inviolable rule that the State should pay for getting the result right and the law right. It must depend on circumstances, but the proviso should be there and availed of more often.

It is sometimes said that, if a respondent in an appeal unsuccessfully tries to support the judge, he cannot be heard to complain against an award of costs against him 'here and below'. Well, to start with why 'below'? It may be just in some circumstances to make him pay the costs above. But most certainly not as a general rule. He has the trial judge in his favour, it may be a moot point, there may be a dissent and it is only rational to debate a debatable point rather than have it go by default.

VAT on Legal Services

Legal costs are, in all conscience, far too high. To add to them VAT at all stages is iniquitous. Had King John (or his Barons) raised the subject at Runnymede or elsewhere, they would have landed in the adjoining Thames. The most of the evil is that it is tax on justice – the fundamental right of every man or woman. The next is that it is an ever-renewing tax: every time you employ a solicitor; every time you go with a solicitor or counsel; every time you go to court.

Over and above that, there are four serious objections:

1. Only those who can 'set out' or otherwise absorb it as business expenses are exempt.

2. Even the legally-aided have to pay it.

3. We do not have to pay it for medical services.

4. Everyone has to pay VAT, both to go to court and again on an appeal.

This is the appalling story of VAT on legal services – an ever accumulating VAT. It should be abolished or at least zero rated – regardless of costs. Everybody should be entitled to consult solicitors or counsel as to his legal rights or obligations without this penal encumbrance. I know many who need legal help but stay away from its taxation.

To tax justice is a plain contradiction in words – it is unjust to tax justice. It is illogical, too – judges, who administer it, do not pay VAT nor do those who administer the courts. And what about the Ministers (the Chancellor himself) or the MPs who legislate? Or the many enforcement officers? What is sauce for the lowly goose should surely be sauce for the golden gander.

I have raised this matter before and am most surprised that neither the Law Society nor the Bar Council have taken it up in any way; nor has anybody else taken it up.

Doubting Thomas

The Gospel, or Lesson, for the 2nd Sunday after Easter relates the story of Doubting Thomas unless he could see for himself absolutely plainly, and feel, Christ's wounds with his hands, he would not believe. Blessed are they who cannot see or feel but nevertheless believe, etc. There is a lesson for all of us, and for judges, lawyers and juries in this. To find truth, what do you need?

In the law, our standards of proof are (1) in criminal cases 'sureness' – the more favoured formula with judges now, rather than 'beyond all reasonable doubt'; (2) in civil cases, 'the balance of probabilities' (which can be just 51 per cent to 49 per cent to tip the scales of justice).

How, with judge alone trials or jury trials, does one find truth? The cynic says 'at the bottom of a well', or by balancing between biases, or by distinguishing between exaggeration on the one side and downright lying on the other. Rarely does the unfortunate judge or jury have 'the proof positive' which Doubting Thomas called for.

On a light – but nevertheless serious – note, I will never forget the incident of the police officer who was asked as the first question in cross-examination by the accused's counsel, 'How did my client look when you arrested him?' This was intended to preface a series of questions to the effect that he looked surprised, shaken, shocked. The police officer completely nailed the accused with the reply, 'He had a guilty look'.

One case gave rise to an incident the like of which I have never heard. A few years ago, a well-known football personality was suing for alleged libel. When John Wilmers, QC, a great friend of mine, who died quite shortly afterwards and at a comparatively early age, rose to cross-examine on behalf of the defendant newspaper, he said, by way of preface, words to this effect, 'I must suggest, Mr X, that for the last two days you have been telling My Lord and the jury a pack of lies'. Now, John Wilmers was an impressive and imposing and formidable figure, but even he could not really have expected the answer he got. 'That is quite right. I have been lying. I am very sorry'.

You will all have cases in mind where truth emerged, either spontaneously, or accidentally; maybe slowly. But it is a fascinating pursuit, the pursuit of truth. And rarely, oh so rarely, do you get it in the way Thomas wanted it.

Personally, I have found, in a long personal and family experience, that cross-examination will rarely, very, very rarely, break the truthful witness – however shifty he looks, however unconvincingly he sounds.

In the daily search for truth, the courts and juries inevitably make mistakes, but perhaps you will agree with me – not that often. Or, put another way, even if they believe somebody who has told them some lies, they often achieve the right overall result. The witness may, for example, have been lying about irrelevancies – for reasons of his own, maybe to hide something in his own past or in his present.

It is easier for judges and lawyers to detect the truth than it is for juries. They have the experience of many years of civil and criminal cases to call upon. They know the reaction of all kinds of men and women in all sorts of circumstances. They know by demeanour, tone of voice and pauses when a lie is being told. Or that is how they feel and others feel. But they must guard against various things – (1) Prejudice against a witness, (2) Dislike of a witness, and (3) The fact that the incredible is often true.

The jury have no such advantages but they bring their own life-long experience of truth and lying to the jury room. It is often wider than the lawyers'; less constricted and less hidebound. They often act as a brake upon lawyers and judges. An additional advantage is that they can pool their resources and discuss things freely without any restriction from the Law of Evidence and little from the law generally. They speak as 12 voices (or 10 in a majority case).

Hired Hit Men

I defended two Hired Hit Men and was the judge in two others. Three were convicted; the fourth, where I was trial judge, was acquitted.

Of all crimes I completely fail to understand is that of a man, for money (often paltry, always by instalments) killing somebody he had never seen before and of whom he knows nothing. It was wickedness at its worst. Long premeditated, long prepared for. He knows nothing of the man's background, family or commitments. He has no quarrel with him, no kind of grievance against him; he is just pointed out to him as the victim.

In the two cases I defended there was really no defence at all, though both pleaded Not Guilty and sought to prove alibis. They were both in the late 1970s and the price one got was £2,000 (£750 before the killing, £1,250 after) and the other got £1,000 (payable as to £500 before and £500 after). Both were in their thirties, but one had a criminal record, but not including violence. The other had no record and looked respectable and honest. One killed a bar manager in a Soho pub, the other a waiter in the East End. Both places were crowded at the time, but in each case the Prosecution had difficulty in getting witnesses – because of fear of possible consequences. All was arranged by a local gang chief, of the type who never killed or maimed himself and had a good security guard.

Both men were convicted and given the mandatory life sentences. I believe that such people should not be paroled for a very long time.

The first Hit Man trial I conducted as a judge was of a man who pleaded Guilty to four Hit murders and others. He 'grassed' to the police in a very big way and became known as 'The Super Grass'. So perilous was his position with the underworld that I acceded to the joint application of Crown and defence that he be shielded in the dock by large boards and that the upstairs public gallery be shut.

Wanting him as they did for further information and cases, the Crown pressed me (as did the defence) to say something which would help him to fairly early release. I absolutely refused to do so and passed six life sentences upon him, saying, 'This is a confirmed and highly dangerous killer.'

The other case I tried was a Hit Man case of murder of an Amusement arcade manager. The police had very great difficulty in getting witnesses. The arcade was relatively empty at the time, and the youths in it pretended that they were so engrossed in their play that they did not see what happened. Moreover the manager was standing in the middle of the Hall and was able to be shot from near the door.

The police, however, managed to piece up a case, relying principally on the 'grassing' of the get-away driver, over whom they had some hold.

The Crown witnesses, such as they were, were good; the 'grassing' driver especially good. The accused did not give evidence. I am afraid in my summing up that I went a lot further about that than a judge should.

In three-quarters of an hour the jury were back with a finding of Not Guilty. Like so many of us they did not like 'grasses'. The same is true in Spy Cases which I have done. Juries do not like – or trust – double agents – those who have come over to us from the other side.

The Halsbury Handicap Hurdle at Haydock

(By Our Racing Correspondent)

Because of the generosity of our legal institutions a unique racing event is to be held at Haydock next Saturday week. It is the £100,000 Halsbury Handicap Hurdle, confined to horses with legal names. Changing of name by Deed Poll or otherwise is not allowed.

There are at present 12 definite runners. Home stables provide 5 – Alibi, Arson, Copyright Contender, Wilful Contempt and Restraint of Trade. All good horses and in with a chance. Ireland produces three – Lying Witness, Partial Jury and Excessive Damages. They are not coming this distance for nothing. A close watch should be kept on all three.

Australia and America provide one each – Waltzing Judge and I Object. I'd expect at least one of them to defray the cost of their trip plus.

France are producing a good one from M Heal's money spinning stables – Juge Extraordinaire. Ignore the three last previous outings. All could be preparation for this great coup.

Lastly there is Latvian lawyer, who is certainly coming a long way. All we know of him is that he was second in the Helsinki Hurdle three months ago but of course one does not know the standard of the opposition. The only advice to give is to Watch Him.

The Monday after The Race.

Who gave you the 1-2-3 in Saturday's big Race? Our Racing Correspondent.

1. Latvian Lawyer   50-1 'Watch Him'.
2. Juge Extraordinaire   10-1 'Ignore the three last'.
3. Lying Witness   12-1 'Not coming this distance for nothing'.

Change

If you are getting change for a £20 or £10 note and are deluged with a mass of silver coins Beware: count your change. Because this is a familiar method of fraud, especially where there are impatient crowds behind you. You could easily find yourself under-changed by 50p or a £1 in the mass of silver which descends on you.

I once prosecuted for London Transport a ticket collector from a mid-London Underground Station. He had been under suspicion for some time. On this occasion there was an Inspector on the platform and a man complained to him that he had been counting his change and found that the ticket collector had under-changed him 50p on a £10 note.

It was rush-hour but the inspector accompanied by the man went upstairs and immediately closed the ticket collector's booth and directed passengers to the opposite booth. He asked the collector when he came on duty and was told an hour before.

The inspector then went through the issuing machine and the till. He found two 50p coins in the till in excess of the tickets sold and two £10 notes. He charged him with stealing two 50p coins, to which the collector replied, 'You can always make mistakes at rush-hours, especially with notes.' The inspector put him off duty indefinitely.

Ten days later I attended to prosecute at Bow Street before a Stipendiary Magistrate and he was represented by counsel. He was charged with stealing the two 50p coins. He pleaded Not Guilty.

We called two witnesses, the man and the inspector. We accepted that the accused was sixteen years on the railway and had no criminal record.

When he went into the box he admitted the deficiencies but said it was all a mistake; at rush periods you had to do things in a hurry and when people irritatingly produced notes for a 25p fare you had to act quickly in the interests of the waiting crowd you could push the wrong button and take too little or too much – out of the till.

I asked him a few questions, 'Have you ever heard of fraud before?', 'No,' he said, with complete lack of conviction.

'Have you ever given people too much change?'

'Sometimes.'

'How often?'

'Perhaps six or seven times in the last year.'

'Did you report it?'

'No.'

'What did you do – make up the deficiencies yourself?'

'Yes.'

'Why?'

'It's too much trouble to report it and you could be blamed.'

The magistrate did not call on his counsel. In a typically laconic way he said, 'Good Record. Long Service. Room for mistake. Both summons dismissed. Costs £25.' I was upset at the result but the inspector cheered me up by saying that unfortunately they'd have to return him to work but he lived in Central London and he would see that he was posted to Cockfosters – just about as far away as you could get from his home.

Clients

Barristers never forget which side they appeared for in cases long gone by – but clients do! I had appeared against the late Humphrey Berkeley (author of that superb book *The Life and Death of Rochester Sneath*) in a long drawn-out action years before. It settled at the door of the Court. Much later I had occasion to write to him – very diffidently – for leave to produce something of his in a book I was writing. I did not in fact expect a reply. I naturally mentioned nothing about the case.

Within a few days I got the following reply –

Dear James Comyn,

Anything you want at any time. I will *never* forget the blistering you gave that little bastard in Court. I often think of it. I am forever grateful to you.

Yours sincerely,

Humphrey Berkeley.

75

His powers of imagination were certainly great – because we never even got into Court at all. Then there was the case of a four-day cruelty divorce battle which I lost for the husband hook, line and sinker. Principally, I think, because he managed to be cruel to the judge a timid little man – in Court! Some three years later I got a heavily embossed Christmas Card of a huge castle from the ex-wife. Scrawling out the printed Lord and Lady Thing, she had penned in the name 'Audrey' and written 'Thank you for getting rid of that awful little man. Do come and stay a weekend here with Phil and myself. I'll keep you posted with our news.' And she did – for about three years.

At an Inner Temple Guest Night a distinguished visitor came up to me – twice. With a handshake like a vice he said, before dinner, 'Delighted to see you again. Often thought of writing to you. That settlement you advised – the one I was reluctant about – has worked wonders. You told me to take half in their shares, and they've shot up. Splendid piece of advice, my dear fella.' I had never seen or heard of him before. I had never advised anyone to take anybody's shares as part of a settlement. After dinner he came up to me again and, in vino, congratulated me once more. With congratulations of course there is no need to disclaim them.

In different vein I had Instructions to act for a young woman who was petitioning for divorce. It was in the awful days of the Discretion (or Indiscretion) Statement where a party had to sign a document setting out his or her infidelities. Once she got the hang of the thing she rolled out name after name. And then at the end she said 'There was one other, but, d'you know, I simply can't think of his name. He was a Captain in the Army.'

'Better call him A. N. Other,' remarked my instructing solicitor, a keen rugby football man. We eventually had to put this man down anonymously as 'an Officer in the Army.'

I thought at first of dealing with the men in groups, but her choices were so various that that proved impossible. I eventually named four at a time – to give some sort of feeling of infrequency. I tucked the Army Officer into the middle of one sentence.

To our surprise the husband did not defend. He had an abundance of grounds!

But there was the judge to cope with.

He just looked at the discretion statement nonchalantly and then incredulously. As he read each line he turned from the Statement to the petitioner, first with bewilderment and then with positive fear.

I did not have to say a word. 'Oh yes, yes,' he said, anxious to get my dangerous client out of his sight.

The Gold Plate

There is no more judicial task more wearisome than deciding between ex-husband and ex-wife who owns what goods and chattels. It is necessarily a case of deliberate and continuous perjury on one side or the other – perhaps both.

The ex-husband says, 'All the cutlery is mine. Poor Aunt Ada gave it to me when she was dying.'

The ex-wife says, 'Nonsense. My cousin Florence gave it to me when she was entering the convent.'

The judge asks hopefully, 'Is there anyone alive who knows about them?'

A chorus of No.

Four pairs of Table Lights (it sounds like a Lot Number). 'Belonged to my Mother,' says the ex-husband.

'Certainly not,' says the ex-wife. 'I bought them myself.'

'Where?', asks counsel.

'I can't remember, it's so long ago.'

Judge to ex-husband, 'Did anyone else see them in your mother's possession?'

'I expect so, My Lord, but they're mostly dead now.'

A writing desk. 'I well remember it. I bought it for £250 at Lezenger before marriage.'

'Would Lezenger have a record?', asked the judge.

'No – unfortunately they closed down about 12 years ago.'

Ex-wife. 'Completely untrue. I always coveted it and my friend Ada Spinks gave it to me for a wedding present.'

Resignedly the judge asks, 'Alive or dead?'

'Dead, My Lord.

A beautiful Buhl cabinet. Says the ex-husband, 'A present to me by my old Squadron-Leader Blair long before marriage, because I gave him some help in his matrimonial affairs.

The judge suppresses a smile.

The ex-wife says, 'Given to me by my Uncle, Fred, years before marriage. You must have seen me move it in after marriage.'

'All you brought in was a lot of dresses and shoes.'

In one case the only worrying item – out of 376 – was a very large pure gold plate, valued at £15,000. It was brought into Court with due solemnity and having been shown round was placed on the nervous Registrar's desk.

'To whom does that belong?', his counsel asked the ex-husband.

'To me,' he said, 'a present from my father for my 21st birthday.'

'A rather unconventional gift, wasn't it,' I said.

'I was surprised to get it but he was an unconventional man. I was his only child.'

The ex-wife burst into floods of tears and kept saying, 'My mother, my mother, my poor dear mother.'

His counsel asked him, 'Where did your father get it?'

'I think from my grandfather.'

'Did you see it before it was presented to you?'

'Yes once. He kept it in a large safe he had.'

'When did you take it away?'

'That day. And I put it in a safe of my own.'

'Did your wife see it?'

'Oh yes. It was she who persuaded me to hang it over the mantelpiece in the study.' Under cross-examination he was asked if he insured the goods in his flat.

'Not the gold plate. Too expensive.'

'Even when you say your wife got you to exhibit it?'

'No.'

'And when you went away on holidays, what happened?'

'I put it back in the safe.'

'Did your wife have a key to the safe?'

'No. I had the only key.'

I interrupted. 'Is there anyone you can call to support your evidence?'

'No,' he said, unfortunately not.'

I was trying the items piece by piece, so the ex-wife – still crying – was the next witness.

'Who owns the gold plate?', her counsel asked.

'I do. A present from my dear mother gave it to me before my previous marriage.'

I came in again, 'So you were previously married – did you get any of the chattels claimed here from your previous marriage?'

'No. '

'Have you any brothers or sisters?'

'Three brothers, two sisters.'

'Did your mother give them anything valuable?'

'Yes – but not as valuable as this.'

'Why you?'

'Well she had to give it to somebody in the family and she chose me.'

'Did you tell any of your brothers and sisters about it?'

There was a long pause. Then she said, 'No I didn't. It would have caused jealousy.'

She said her mother kept it in a safe, she removed it a few days later and left it with a friend now dead – who had a safe. She left it there during her first marriage (10 minutes of Why from everyone), brought it round to this ex-husband's flat and Yes she did ask him to exhibit it. After all it was hers. No – she hadn't given any thought to Insurance.

Asked by her ex-husband's counsel where her mother had got it from she said she did not know.

'Was it her mother's richest possession?', she was asked in cross-examination. Hesitantly she said, 'Yes, but she had a number of good pictures.'

'Could she spare £15,000 for it?'

'I expect it was many years ago and the price has gone up.'

'Did she attend auctions?'

'Oh yes.'

We then passed on to all the other disputed items, and they took no less than 4 days to try. All except the Gold Plate were relatively easy to try and came to roughly 50-50, a division the parties could have come to without all the costs of litigation. It came also to disbelieving them half and half. I reserved Judgment to think principally about the Gold Plate.

My first thought was to give a Judgment of Solomon about it; to order that it be sold and the proceeds divided between both sides.

But in the end I decided to award it to the ex-husband. His version was the more plausible. I distrusted her weeping. And I found it unlikely that she had been chosen out of three brothers and two sisters for such an exceptionally valuable gift – five equally close relatives to whom she never spoke of it.

Both sides asked for costs. I said that where there had been so much lying on both sides I would award no costs.

Roger Gray's client

The late Roger Gray QC of our Chambers had a consultation with Spike Milligan.

Clement escorted Mr Milligan to Roger's door, whereupon the client took a running leap across the floor, jumped on to his desk, leant backwards and eyed Roger from underneath his trousers.

The solicitor, about to do the introducing, was shaken rigid. But imperturbable as ever Roger, leant forwards, grasped the client's hand and said, 'The chairs are unoccupied, Mr Milligan – wouldn't you feel more comfortable in one?'

The Coward

For cowardice in battle
They took him out at dawn
A man who walked with stumbling steps
So frightened and forlorn.

Some lies are unforgivable,
And some deserve our praise,

The General took out his pen
And sought a fitting phrase.

In writing to the parents
He very simply said,
'I regret your son is missing
And we must presume him dead.'

The General fell thinking –
'Yes, cowards they must die;
But what about the undiscovered ones,
The cowards such as I?'

'Dear Sir – Unless'

Box & Cox
Solicitors
4 Goose House
Gosling Lane
CHICHESTER
West Sussex
1997

To: Mr John Smith
Back at: 3A Tooting Terrace
           Tooting
           LONDON SW

Dear Ex Client,
You owe us £9,000 and your freedom.

Unless you pay us within a week, we will take such steps as will amaze you.

We have twice sent you detailed bills but apart from your initial fee of £1,000 you have paid nothing.

Here is a summary, including VAT and credit:

December 1 1996

To visiting you at Maidstone Prison when you said you didn't think you could oppose extradition to the USA for murdering the Ambassador of the Mongolia Islands. On reminding you that capital punishment still existed for this, and that a reprieve was unlikely, you changed your mind and asked us to retain leading QC and Junior.

£500

December 2 1996

To worrying about your case all that night (time and a half).

£500

December 3 1996

To briefing Mr Box QC and Mr Cox to represent you.

£250

December 4 1996

At your request visiting your wife to impart news. She was much distressed at your change of mind as she told us she had plans to remarry on your execution.

£250

January 2, 1997

Extradited.

£2,500

January 4 1997

Appeal to QB Divisional Court. Presiding judge finds irreparable flaw in the documents against you. Extradition lifted and you are released.

£2,500

Counsel advise you not to go to the USA or the Mongolias again or to travel by USA or Mongolian ship or aircraft.

January 7 1997

Visited you at Maidstone Prison on charge of murdering your
wife because of her reaction above. You state you are guilty.

£1,500

March 28, 1997

You are surprisingly acquitted of murder. Police contemplat-
ing charging you with bribery of jurors and witnesses,
perjury, corruption etc. We cease to act.

£2,000

£10,000

Less £1,000

£9,000

Disposing of Bodies

Many murderers leave the victim's body where it lies (for example,
Mr Thompson in the Bywaters and Thompson case, 1922-23).
Others make hasty and suspicious burials (Miss Barlow in the
Seddon case, 1912; Armstrong, the solicitor, of his wife, 1921).
Still others have buried bodies in wild and remote places (The
'Moors Murders', 1966). Murderers have sought to drown their
victim (10-year-old Moira Tinsley by Nodder in the River Idle,
1987;) Gifford disposing of his two parents over a cliff-top into
the sea, 1952; Camb pushing a young actress out of the porthole
(when the Durban Castle was at sea, 1952). A number have literally
destroyed, or sought to destroy, their victims. Some of the best
remembered cases are outlined below.

'The Body Snatchers', Burke and Hare (1829) escaped execution by turning King's Evidence. They took the bodies they
'snatched', and later of those they murdered, to the famous
Scottish anatomist, Dr Knox, who paid them between £7.50 and
£14 per body. After the trial feelings ran high against Dr Knox

and he had to flee Edinburgh. He died, an obscure General Practitioner, in Hackney, London.

On Guy Fawkes Night 1930, Alfred Arthur Rouse burned his car on a deserted country road in Northamptonshire, having picked up 'a down and out'. His intention was that the remains of the other man would be taken as his own and that he would disappear completely from his troubles and difficulties. He was nearly successful, but two young men returning home late saw the blazing car and saw a man (the registered owner) hurrying away. This led directly to Rouse's capture.

Crippen (1910) destroyed the whole of his wife's body, apart from a small piece of stomach, which later confirmed her identification.

John George Haig (1949), 'The Acid Bath Murderer', virtually disposed of Mrs Durand-Deacon in an acid bath at Crawley, Surrey. But just enough evidence, including teeth, remained to identify her as a fellow guest at a hotel in South Kensington, London. He murdered, and probably similarly treated, at least five other people as well, all for personal gain. He claimed in the end to be a vampire or ghoul, drinking his victims' blood. Haig's defence did not succeed and he was executed. Extraordinarily as the case was, there was a similar case in France in 1925 (Georges Sarret)l of which Haig may have read.

In France probably the greatest murderer of all was Henri Desire Landau (1922). It is said that he murdered 300 women (probably a gross exaggeration). That there was a very large number is clear from a note book of his containing the names of 'missing women'. Landau was a swindler and seducer who obtained names through advertisements, then brought the more opulent ones to his house at Gambais and disposed of them by pushing them into a stove, thereby reducing them to ashes. So efficiently was this done that it was impossible to identify any of the women. Landau was convicted on the evidence of the stove, the note book and various garments.

Another famous French murderer was Dr Marcel Petiot (1946) who killed at least 27 people (but boasted of 63). The majority of his victims arrived during the German Occupation of France between 1940 and 1944. He posed as one who could get people to safety out of France – telling the 'escapees' to bring all their cash and valuables. He lolled his victims by injections or gas; then, after treatment in quick-lime, they were incinerated in a furnace at his house. Eventually the smoke attracted the attention of a neighbour who reported it. His defence was, ingeniously, that he was a Resistance leader helping refugees and that those he killed were Germans or collaborators. The jury rejected this patriotic pretence.

Herman W. Mudgett (real name Holmes) (1896) was an American insurance swindler and mass murderer. Holmes was finally trapped through the murder of a man called Pitzer and his three children. It was disclosed at the trial that his house in Chicago had a laboratory, with a bloodstained dissecting table, a stove, a sound-proof vault and quick-lime. His victims were estimated at about 12 people.

One of the most notorious cases in British history is that of John Reginald Halliday Christie (1953), of 10 Rillington Place, North Kensington, London. During the Second World War he was a 'respectable' special constable but in fact lolled, raped and had post-death intercourse (necrophilia) with prostitutes, whom he buried in bomb craters. He and his wife gave damning evidence against Timothy John Evans (1950) when on trial for the murder of his baby. Evans blamed Christie for the murder of his wife and baby but was disbelieved and was subsequently hanged. Three years later, Christie was tried for the murder of his wife and was convicted and hanged. The bodies or skeletons of three women were found in an opening behind wallpaper in the house, the body of Mrs Christie was found under the floor and two skeletons of war time murders were found in the garden. Christie admitted killing Mrs Evans but not the baby. Later, in trying to prove insanity, Christie claimed to have committed over 20 murders – which could well be true.

Just

Just for a handful of silver he left us,
Eleventh the hour for returning his Brief,
Of valuable services thus he bereft us
Causing us chaos surpassing belief.

Many years now since that handful of silver
Instructing Solicitors think of it yet,
They've never sent him a Brief (for returning)
Instructing Solicitors never forget.

In Two Docks

In Dublin a young woman accused of stealing valuables from a relative tried to show her contempt for the Court by standing with her back to the Court when called upon to plead. Eventually the judge ordered her back to the cells, entered a plea of Not Guilty and told her that she could listen to the proceedings in her cell.

Earlier, at the Exeter Assizes, in England, she tried the same tactics with Mr Justice Hugh Park. He said to her, 'This case is scheduled for three days. If that is the way you want to behave go on doing so. But if you decide to behave more conventionally you can sit down but only if and when I tell you to.' She grew tired of her antics but the judge did not let her sit down for the remainder of the day.

She was a good tennis player and when in jail in the West of Ireland qualified to meet a girl from Mountjoy Jail in Dublin in (would you believe it?) the final of the Women's Jail Competition Singles. This was arranged to take place at Portlaoise Prison in the Irish Midlands. This prompted a retired Colonel from Killiney, Co Dublin, to write to one of the national papers as follows:—

'I strongly favour neutral grounds for Finals, but as a tax-payer I resent double trips for the finalists of a Women Convicts' tennis match. Why not let the title be shared? And might we be informed if the same process pertains in The Men's Singles, The Men's

Doubles, The Women's Doubles – and of course The Mixed Doubles? Am I partly sponsoring all these events?'

Indecent Exposure

It is an offence for a man to expose his person with intent to insult a female; commonly called 'flashing' in legal circles.

This is fairly prevalent. From my experience of some twenty cases of it (only about five successful) I am persuaded that (a) it is usually occasional, not frequent; (b) it is a peculiar sexual aberration which does not lead on to other sexual offences; and (c) it is virtually impossible to cure.

A surprising feature about it is that it is usually committed by otherwise respectable law-abiding men – and predominantly in the early morning hours or early evening.

It is really a form of sickness – with the 'pleasure' going to the man and no actual desire to insult the woman.

I think that too many cases are brought about it. The more innocuous ones would be better met by a severe warning.

Often even acquittals are met by pieces in the papers. I once had a Housemaster at a well-known Public School, rightly acquitted, prominently displayed – and identified – in many of the next morning's papers. Inevitably he lost his job.

A cleric client of mine, who was convicted, was consumed with shame, and although my Instructing Solicitor and I told him that he had a good chance on appeal – which he had – he immediately began to threaten suicide. 'The shame of it, the shame of it,' he kept saying. 'How can I face my Parish again?' We took him to coffee and managed to calm him down a bit. But he kept referring to suicide and we both told him not to be silly, that there was a lot to live for and that suicide was sinful.

Unfortunately neither of us took the threat seriously, and I remember saying to him 'Your conscience is clear and that is all that matters.'

If we had taken him seriously (a man with no previous charge, who should never have been arrested) we would have done something about it, such as bring him to an Anglican priest, but he was obviously level headed and reasonable, so we left him after about forty minutes. Within two hours we heard that he had stabbed himself to death.

Nevermore did I tolerate a client's suicide threats without taking some steps to prevent them.

A Birmingham Riddle

When reading the judge's papers the night before I found them so complicated that I was afraid no jury could possibly understand them. Two of the three accused were alleged to have posed as mortgage brokers and to have established high-sounding companies. They then set up an involved scheme where unfortunate householders who found themselves unable to keep up their mortgage payments sold them to nominees and later bought them back from the nominees on stringent terms. The nominees were themselves under their contract. The third accused only took part in the scheme once.

The scheme involved misrepresentations and sometimes forged documents to get them mortgages from Building Societies different to those originally concerned, on various properties and it was alleged that the two main accused pocketed the money. On one occasion the scheme went wrong and the first Accused had to pose both as nominee and as a person interested in getting a mortgage.

It came down in the end to criss-cross defrauding of householders and Building Societies. All pleaded Not Guilty and prosecuting counsel tardily said that it would take him some time to open the case and go through the documents.

I looked carefully at the jury. Eleven men and one woman. Prosecuting counsel was good but after half an hour I saw tremors of complete mystification on the faces of most of the jury. I remembered the Irish story of a foreman of the jury saying when they got into their room 'Can anyone tell me what this case is all about?'

The opening lasted all that day and into the next, with stupor and mounting bewilderment creeping through nearly all the jury. Then at twenty to two the next afternoon, my clerk being at lunch, I went back to Court to collect a book.

When he came back he was laughing and told me that there was the whole jury, 20 minutes ahead of schedule, some in their box, some sitting on chairs, and they were being harangued in a broad Irish accent by the one lady juror. He heard her saying it was all very simple, just listen to her.

It was plain sailing after that. On one occasion she actually corrected prosecuting counsel in his opening.

After nine days all three were convicted of everything – within an hour.

There was a beautiful smile on the face of the lady and contented smiles shown in the faces of the other jurors as they heard that the two ring-leaders had previous convictions for insurance frauds.

Arson

Arson is strangely enough one of the easiest crimes to detect. Insurance companies have investigators of long experience, accustomed to dealing with many arsons as against the one or two committed by the arsonist. The police, too, have their experts. To them Fire Does Not Consume All.

I once had to defend a stockbroker on a charge of Arson of his car and claiming by deception compensation for stolen goods. Through having an excellent record he was on bail pending trial.

The disturbing thing to find was that he was in a shaky state financially, largely due to speculating in shares and horses. That is a familiar background to arson.

His story – backed up by his wife – was that they went to bed one night in their country cottage and in the morning found that they had been broken into, a number of things had gone and his expensive car was missing.

He reported the matter immediately to the police and his insurance company. The police found the car next day in a field about twenty miles away, completely burnt out except for its wrecked and tangled iron-work.

The police and fire insurance assessors started work on the car and the cottage.

They found nothing worthwhile in the car or around it except for rubber boot marks at a muddy part of the gate, similar to those which the accused had at home. There was more that fixed their suspicion about him in the cottage. The point of entry to the cottage was from the garage and it looked as if the garage doors had been opened from the inside, it seemed as if the side door had been prised open by an instrument or instruments (of which the accused had many in his carpentry set) and there were no signs of any foot-prints in the house or garage, apart from those of the accused and his wife.

The wife had a smaller car, which was parked in front.

Why, asked the police, have a second car at a country cottage? Our client replied that she was probably going to stay on for a few days. They located a man and his girlfriend seeing two cars, one large and one small, near the field gate.

They also found out about his financial position.

No charge came for about a fortnight, which was probably due to careful consideration in the Director of Public Prosecutions' Office. Then the accused was charged, but his wife was not.

At the preliminary hearing before the magistrate I tried to get the case thrown out, on the basis that a lot of little grains did not make a pile; and that, as grave as the charge was, so heavier was the burden of proving it. He rejected it.

At the Old Bailey after the prosecution case ended I tried the same tactic by submitting No Case to Answer. He refused it. I then called the Accused, who was excellent. When asked as the first question in cross-examination, 'Why didn't you or your wife hear anything?', he said, 'That surprises me because we're neither of us heavy sleepers.' The wife, who was not in Court, said the same.

I got into slight trouble with the judge in re-examining by saying, 'If you were going to burn anything why not the cottage? That would burn everything, the car included.' I called the wife and a fire assessor. The latter was a mistake. He was good in my hands but the Crown had a list of cases where his evidence had been rejected. My proof said four times in over forty cases. To prosecuting counsel he reluctantly admitted to some twenty. After speeches the judge summed-up, completely fairly and if anything rather in favour of the accused.

The jury were out for hours but could not agree. The accused was remanded for a re-trial, bail continued.

At the re-trial the only difference was that we called a new fire assessor. But again after a long adjournment the jury disagreed.

Assuming that the Crown would say that they did not want to proceed further, the judge adjourned for a short time. It is possible – but rare – to prosecute a third time, and of course the decision rests with the Crown. My opponent told me that he would need the night to take Instructions. I said, 'Very well but I will bring out that there have been 2 disagreements.' Next morning he came back and told the judge that the Prosecution did not wish to proceed further – and the judge formally acquitted him.

The claim was worth about £30,000 and the insurance company still refused to pay; the criminal proceedings were no bar to them and they could contest it in civil procedures. After about four months he consulted me about bringing a civil claim. I warned him that it would amount to a re-trial before a judge alone and that no less than 24 people had disagreed about it, for reasons unknown. He decided to go on.

The document of defence followed the prosecution case – fraud, arson, wilful deception. About half an hour before we were due in court my opponent asked me if we could talk. 'My people', he said, 'are prepared to settle this for £10,000 and £2,000 towards costs; no bargaining.'

I was surprised. I thought it might be the two disagreements which had influenced them. 'I'll put it to my client.'

I was more than surprised at his reaction, which I expected to be All or Fight. He immediately said, 'I'll take it.' I pointed out that it was about one-third of his claim and limited his costs. 'No', he said, 'I'll take it.' I pointed out that although they had said No there might be room for bargaining. He said, 'No, I'll take it as it stands.'

Being now wary of everything in the case I asked him –

unusually – to sign a statement on the back-sheet of my Brief, saying 'I voluntarily accept the defendant's offer of £10,000 and £2,000 towards costs in full settlement of this action. The decision is mine alone.' He duly signed and I got my instructing solicitor to witness it.

I have often wondered about the case since.

Neighbours

My father regularly advised neighbours in our district of Tara, County Meath, Ireland, helped them to understand long official documents, told them how to reply to letters, and occasionally appeared for them in Court. All of course for nothing. I took over his role when he died.

The stories I tell here cannot be identified because they are long past and the people are dead.

What my experience at home at Tara taught me – even more forcibly than at the Bar – was that a barrister is perhaps a quarter of the time a lawyer and the rest of the time a guide, philosopher and friend. For example, there was no law at all in interpreting official documents; nothing but experience of hundreds of them. Many years later, still finding the same kind of documents around I wonder why it happens. They could be so easily simplified and shortened. Can it really be thought that elderly widows and aged farmers from small farms will begin to understand them?

One of the first 'cases' I had was for an odd-job man, who produced an estimated Income Tax demand. I said, 'That's only estimated. You can appeal it.'

'It's the first I've ever received', he said. 'I was thinking of sealing it up, writing DEAD all across the front and posting it back to them. I don't want to join their scheme.'

I couldn't help laughing. 'You'll be surrounded by inspectors if you do that. Let's look at the figures.'

Poor man, he had no records of any kind, he had no bank account (he kept the money in the house) and there was not one single document to support earnings or expenses. I told him that there was over £400 at stake and he should use an accountant. He reluctantly agreed to do so. I gave him a couple of names. He came round later to say it was all cleared up and he owed nothing. 'Only thing,' he said, 'is I'm in that bloody Scheme forever. The missus will have to cook up some books now.'

A daily-woman came down one evening to ask my advice about her husband. 'He's in the Mental Hospital for the second time now,' she said, 'but threatening to come out. If I manage to get him in a third time does that mean an end to the marriage?' Suppressing any laughter I said, 'Ma'am you've been watching too much of the Horse Show. Three faults in marriage doesn't mean you're out.'

She finally said resignedly, 'If I kept putting him in and taking him out how often would I have to do it to get rid of him?'

I replied, 'You're playing the wrong game. When you have something directly against him you'd better go to a solicitor.'

A close friend of mine named John burst in to see me late one evening. He was in a state for John Jameson, of which I gave him two quick doses. 'What's the matter?', I asked.

'After five years I've been caught, well nearly caught,' he said, 'you know my old blue van. I haven't taxed it, you see, for five years. I use a Guinness label as a disc and I never come out in it until it's dark. Earlier this evening a garda came up to my mother about a missing cow and I know he saw the van in the yard; he actually looked at it, because it's very distinctive.'

I interrupted, 'Well you're alright so far, John. It wasn't on a public road.

'That's true', he said, 'but they'll watch me.'

A thought suddenly occurred to me. 'How did you get down here this evening?'

'The blue van of course.'

'You are a bloody fool, John. Uninsured, unlicensed, false pretences. Five years of it. You leave that van here tonight, I'll run you home and tomorrow I'll see to it that old van is broken up.'

As we talked it was clear that, like so many otherwise reasonable people, he did not really appreciate the vital importance of insurance.

He was right about the garda. He had taken in the details of the van. A week later he and a fellow officer called to see John, 'What's happened to the van, sir?' 'I've had it destroyed. It was on its last legs.

'That was a very good idea, sir.'

As they walked away the other officer said, 'I suppose you kept the tax disc. You could you know get a refund on it.'

The local police are kind and tactful. They know when a blind eye can properly be closed. But they got very, very tired indeed of a close neighbour of mine who was always ringing them up or calling in to see them with a series of spurious or trivial complaints. When they were courteous he was abusive. Now, he farmed on both sides of a narrow road and frequently drove his tractor from one side to the other. He also drove light agricultural machinery in the same way. Neither the tractor nor the machinery were licensed or insured. One day two garda cars stationed themselves behind trees one below his yard entrance and the other above. It was morning feeding time and in due course he came on to the road with his tractor and a load of hay.

With perfect precision, just when he was in the middle of this narrow road both sets of Gardaí pounced – no licence, no insurance, middle of a main road. He fumed and shouted but to no avail.

He came to see me and wanted me to defend him when the summons came on. I said (with personal unwillingness) that I would if he instructed a solicitor (whom he would have to pay). We decided to plead Not Guilty and try to make some technical points, as well as bringing out the comparative triviality of the offences.

It was a hot summer's day but the client was shivering. Then the case was called and the police played their golden card. The prosecuting inspector said, 'We do not wish to proceed in this case, sir, but would oppose costs.'

'Costs not asked for', I said.

The garda never again had any trouble from my client.

The Dissenting Judgment

Lord Justice Starch and Lord Justice Moon had just given judgments dismissing the plaintiff's appeal with costs. Then came a dissenting judgment by Lord Justice Heron. Lord Justice Heron. I am the only Chancery judge who has heard this distinctly Chancery Case and I am in the unfortunate position of disagreeing entirely with both my learned brothers in the result they have arrived at and the differing reasons which have led them to it.

I agree that the point is new and important but I fail to see why it should have taken as long as 13 days before us and eight days before the trial judge. The presence of the learned Attorney-General on behalf of the Crown naturally adds something to the length of a case but not to the extent I have indicated.

Now before turning to the faults at law I would like to put firmly on record my view that our law is bedevilled by rules.

Exceptions to the rules and then exceptions to the exceptions. This is just such a case, a creature of statutes.

We are concerned with the Debris Land and Premises Act 1895 – Just over 100 years ago. Section 1 provides that any debris land or premises can be taken over by the Crown on notice given and if called for Public Enquiry. Needless to say there is no definition of debris.

The plaintiff, Mr Cavah, says that his land and building at Walthamstow are not and never were debris. The Attorney-General and the defendant counsel take the preliminary point that he should have gone – at any rate first – to the stipulated enquiry.

Having considered series of photographs and the evidence before the trial judge I am convinced that the plaintiff is right; neither his land nor his premises are or were debris, which I take to mean a wreckage or a ruin. They are certainly going that way but are a long way short of it.

Land and premises are primarily Chancery Division matters and that is why I regard this as really a Chancery question.

As to the preliminary objection I see two answers – one, why go to an enquiry if you are not a debris-holder?, and two, the power of the Court is nowhere ruled out.

That means in my Judgment that the plaintiff succeeds on his very first point. But in case this matter should go higher I ought to deal with the exceptions and the Exceptions to the exceptions.

Section 2 of the Act says that section 1 shall not apply if the land or premises have been put to useful use during the three months preceding the said matter.

This plaintiff had files on the premises, and to such lengths have we gone this Court spent two days inspecting them. In my opinion they came within that horrible phrase 'useful use.' True they are of no use to the Learned Attorney-General but they are to the plaintiff. As to the land he had a donkey on it for over a year. But it is said that the donkey, during the relevant three months, broke out on two occasions, one over-night. Unlike my brothers I pay no attention to that. It was his paddock at all times. And animals stray temporarily from their homes for a variety of reasons.

If it arose I would therefore find for the plaintiff on this exception.

Lastly, section 3, for some reason which I cannot fathom (it is a judge's duty not to fathom but to decide) says that the storing of machinery will not count as 'useful use.' Mine not to reason why. Counsel against the plaintiff put forward various lists of so-called machinery broken down central heating, a defunct washing-machine, a cut-off telephone, an electric light system which no longer lit – and in the field a working trough and a broken down car. That is not a complete list but covers the best they could devise. As I understand my learned brothers they picked various different items as constituting 'machinery.' To my mind it is stretching imagination too far to call a disused telephone or an ancient water trough 'machinery.' And the same goes for the rest of this so-called list.

I would therefore hold that the plaintiff does not come within this exception to an exception.

I would allow his appeal on all grounds, with costs.

Leave to Appeal to the House of Lords.

Company Fraud

I rarely prosecuted; I much preferred to defend. But in one case at Exeter Assizes I appeared for the Crown against Hugh Park QC (later Mr Justice Park) in an extremely odd company fraud case.

There has long been a compulsory retiring age for company directors, but unbelievably there was not then (and still not) any age for becoming a director or company official.

Mr X and his wife under her maiden name formed a company giving itself the widest activities (from market gardening to engineering) and were the two accused, charged with widespread company frauds of nearly a quarter of a million pounds over a period of three years.

They had two fellow directors – their son of ten and their daughter of eight. The Company Secretary was their other son, aged six. None of this appeared anywhere until the police started their investigations. Such papers as they found were letters to 'The secretary' and 'Minutes' signed by him in a juvenile scrawl. They also found that Mrs X had registered under her maiden name at her aunt's address in Wales and the daughter had changed her name to accord with her mother's and was registered at the same address. Meantime of course the whole family had been living together cosily – and prosperously – a few miles outside Exeter.

Father and mother had defrauded hundreds of people of thousands of pounds by a fake mail-order business based on a false name under a PO Box Number at a nearby town, by borrowing from banks on cleverly forged share certificates, by floating dud companies, by buying up old people's homes and property – then selling them at a large profit – and by a variety of devious other ways.

They pleaded Guilty to a number of specimen charges and when I told the astonished judge about the true constitution of the company he was astonished. 'I suppose', he said, 'a babe in arms could be secretary of any company.'

'Nothing to stop him, My Lord', I replied, 'except that somebody would have to guide his handwriting at first.'

'There would be no trouble about that, Mr Comyn, ' he said, 'given the sort of forgery that seems rampant in this case.'

I then told him briefly about the various charges and his astonishment grew. 'What fools people are', he said. 'Sending good money to a Post Office number for something they probably don't want and which they never get.'

When I got to the forged share certificates he asked to see one and I handed up a bundle. Having looked at them he said 'I must say they're good, but do you tell me that the three banks you've mentioned don't take any steps to check with the registrar that these people whom they hardly know – have in fact got such very large holdings?'

'I'm afraid not, My Lord, but I expect they will from now on.'

'And some people', he said with past recollection, 'have to pretty well pledge their house to get a loan of £50.

'Tell me about these dud companies, Mr Comyn, how many were there?' 'Six, My Lord. They were very grandiosely advertised in papers and by brochures. I'll hand some up to Your Lordship.' I handed him up all 6 brochures and 2 advertisements. He looked through them and then glanced at me in silence for a moment. Then he said, 'And none of these high-sounding enterprises ever existed?'

'No, My Lord.'

'And how much did the unfortunate public subscribe to them?'

'Just short of a hundred thousand pounds', I replied.

'Good Heavens', he said.

I passed quickly through the other details which it was necessary for him to know, and I called the officer in charge of the case. He confirmed that both accused had previous good characters, that they had been in custody for 4 months pending trial, that the children were being properly looked after by their paternal grandmother, and that the whole matter had come to light by accident. The wife of a local landowner sent £75 by cheque to the PO Box Number for clothes she had seen advertised. They never came. She got the paid cheque from her bank, it was endorsed to another payee, she tried to trace it but couldn't and then went to the police, who, after nearly a year's investigation, unearthed all the matters charged.

'Had nobody else been to the police about any of these matters before?' Asked the judge.

'So far as we could ascertain', replied the inspector, 'there had been about a dozen complaints by police, throughout the country, but for one reason or another nothing transpired.'

He then illustrated what his force had found, as I had opened it.

My opponent cross-examined him about the background of his two clients, that the husband served well in the Army during the War, that he had found life difficult afterwards and had 'drifted' into crime.

The judge's only intervention was about the word 'drifted.'

'Drifted', he said, 'what an odd word. It seems to me he positively dived into it.'

The defence had no witnesses to call, and with hardly anything to go on but good character and the disruption of a young family their counsel made a very good speech in mitigation. I expected a term of imprisonment for each of about five years. However, calling it 'a wicked and widespread fraud, continued with no regard for the victims, the judge said, 'No term of imprisonment could possibly punish you both sufficiently. I'm satisfied you were the ringleader X and you will go to prison for seven years. And you Mrs X will go to prison for five and a half years.

Leonard MacNally – or M'Nally (1752–1820)

The most detested person in Irish and English history is the informer, and the most detested of them is one who betrays his profession and his clients. Such a one was Leonard MacNally (1752–1820), the only one at the Irish Bar who regularly broke his client's trust for money from the Dublin Castle Prosecuting Authorities. He systematically passed them on information obtained from clients and whole briefs for them to copy.

He was known and respected as an honourable member of the Bar during the whole of the turbulent legal times from 1794 until his death twenty-six years later; especially at the time of the innumerable prosecutions after the 1798 Rising. His base conduct was only discovered after his death. He was a close 'friend' of and frequently led by that indomitable defender of prisoners John Philpot Curran (1750–1819) who wrote him affectionate and confidential letters, Curran, the man of whom it was justly said 'refused to be intimidated'. It is thankful that he did not know of his junior's infamy. Mr. Curran used to say that informers were men beyond reason; like Thomas Reynolds (who got 500 guineas for informing the Government of the Rising and giving evidence) and James O'Brien (whose testimony was so wicked that it led to acquittal in no less than sixteen cases of men whose lives depended on his evidence. It was one of Curran's constant complaints that in Ireland it needed only one witness to convict for treason whereas in England it needed two.

It is unknown how many MacNally led to their death, not only the accused but those mentioned in their Briefs. He was the most dangerous of all informers – secret and immune to prosecution. Judging from other bribes to informers he must have done exceedingly well financially over his many years of corruption.

MacNally's powers of deception must have been very great because in the 2-volume Life of Curran by his son William Henry

'. . . and as my client has the mental age of 14, m'lud, may I suggest he be put in an unlocked council children's home?'

Curran (published in 181 9) he praises M'Nally (as he calls him) in the most glowing terms. For example, 'A gentleman in whom the client has always found a zealous and intrepid advocate, and in whom Mr. Curran, from his youth to his latest hour, possessed a most affectionate and trusty friend'. Again, 'For three and forty years M'Nally was the friend of the subject of these pages; and during that long period, uninfluenced by any obligation, more than once at his own personal risk he performed the duties of counsel with the most uncompromising and romantic fidelity.'

These are very good words in the circumstances – 'uninfluenced by any obligations, 'at his own personal risk' and 'with the most uncompromising and romantic fidelity.'

He was a playwright and author. In his youth he wrote Robin Hood and composed The Lass of Richmond Hill.

There are no better words to describe him than The Man Who Killed His Clients – The Infamous Informer.

Malcolm Morris

The late Malcolm Morris was a junior counsel when, in 1950, he defended unfortunate Timothy Evans of 10 Rillington Place for the murder of his baby daughter; a charge of murdering his wife was put back and in the event never took place because he was found guilty on the first charge and was hanged. He was given a posthumous free pardon in 1966. A most important prosecution witness in the Evans case was John Reginald Halliday Christie, also of 10 Rillington Place; his wife too gave Crown evidence. He posed as a respectable man.

One of the most courageous things I have ever heard of at the Bar was Malcolm Morris's attack upon Christie, accusing him explicitly of having murdered the Evans child and Mrs Evans. Despite the hostility of the judge he went on hammering home at the point. Christie as convincing a liar as has ever been before the Courts – emphatically denied the allegations and was helped by a judge who pressed him to bring out his career as a wartime special constable.

It was of course Malcolm's duty to put and reiterate the questions, but not to press them as bravely and resolutely as he did – before a mistaken judge, jury and audience. It was a splendid example for the Bar – when everybody's prejudice was against him.

Three years after Evan's execution (in 1950) Christie was in the same dock as Evans, charged with the murder of Mrs Christie – several other charges of murder of young women being held over pending the result of this trial. He was found Guilty and hanged. He was a mass murderer, mostly of youngish women. He confessed to many murders, including that of Mrs Evans (but not the baby). Some of his confessions went far beyond the ten or so suspected, possibly in order to establish himself as insane, but the confession about Mrs Evans was legitimate. Most of the murders had taken place years before he gave evidence against Evans. Many of them had taken place in wartime, when he was a special constable.

Christie was a sex maniac, invariably cutting off and keeping women's pubic hair and regularly having intercourse with them after death (necrophilia).

It may seem odd to say so but I regard the execution of Evans and Christie as strong arguments against the death penalty. Evans was innocent, and would never have been found guilty if Christie's record were then known. Christie was in my view utterly and completely mad. His record, his behaviour, spread over many years, demonstrates it. He was found to be not insane – within legal limits – by a jury and the Home Office medical specialists. But in ordinary language and by ordinary standards he was, I consider, plainly mad, and on that ground should not have been hanged.

The story also shows that courageous Malcolm Morris was right. It also shows frighteningly – how very many were wrong. Prejudice can be fatal.

Charity

I was lucky enough once to have eight libel briefs for the managing director of a famous company who had been severely and unjustfully criticised in the financial columns of eight national newspapers, for remarks made in his Chairman's report.

Soon after the Writs were issued all eight actions were settled for very substantial amounts plus an agreed statement in Open Court – all at the newspapers' expense, which covered myself and a junior.

They came on at roughly weekly intervals. For every case our client insisted on me saying in Open Court that 'he intends to give the money to charity.'

On about the fourth occasion my junior (Desmond Browne I think) said to me 'Has he ever told you what charity?'

I said 'No – but I think charity in general.'

'I don't, ' he replied, 'I believe charity with him begins at home. ' So I decided to ask him. 'I have no favourite Charity.' he observed, 'but I'm going through them. ' I began to share my junior's suspicion that all this emphasis on charity was 'a good build up.'

For the last three cases we drew the senior judge in town (the usual Tribunal) – Mr Justice Stable. By the last case he was obviously sharing our suspicions about charity, and at the end he said to me (with that naughty smile), 'Mr Comyn your client must be running out of charities to benefit. I have one for him to consider (say) The League for Broken Down Hunters. If he liked I could arrange it myself for him.'

'I will take his instructions, My Lord.'

Turning to the client he shook his head vehemently and murmured to me.

I gave a cough and said 'My Lord he tells me that he is an active member of the League Against Cruel Sports.'

'Yes', reflected the judge, 'I thought he might be. But do tell him if he is stuck for a charity I have a few others tucked up my sleeve. You can always get in touch with me if he wants you to.'

The client never availed himself of the judge's offer.

Nurse Cadden (1956)

Mary Anne (Mamic) Cadden was, in her fifties and sixties, a well-known – indeed infamous abortionist in Dublin. Known in fact throughout Ireland. It all began in 1939 when, with another woman, she was charged with abandoning a six-weeks old child on a roadside near Dunshaughlin in County Meath, at a time when she was running, or purporting to run, a nursing home (mostly maternity cases) in Rathmines, Dublin. The baby survived, but perhaps because of the unusual nature of the case the national newspapers took it up in a big way at all its stages, District Court and Circuit Court (before my uncle Judge Michael Comyn QC). Both accused were attended at trial by throngs of people and they were photographed time and again. Nurse Cadden – she was always known by that name – had a red sports car and at the time was red-haired, and such a car having been seen near the place just before she was easily traced. She was convicted and sentenced to twelve months' imprisonment. Her name, and photographs, were household news – and remained so. There was much gossip, all untrue, about unwanted babies having been found in the gardens and of garda (police) investigations.

This Philadelphia-born woman living in Ireland, faced another charge, in April 6, 1945, of unlawfully using instruments to procure a miscarriage. She was sent to prison for five years. This amply preserved her memory.

Then in 1956 two things happened, when Nurse Cadden had given up the Nursing Home and moved to a room in a boarding house at Hume Street, near St. Stephen's Green. First, she was charged with sending a letter threatening to kill her husband if he tried to have her evicted by shooting him and putting 'the butcher's knife to the handle in his stomach.' This was brought out by the Defence at her trial for murder of a woman in an illegal operation at Ely Place. It was brought out, like her two trials, to give the jury a full picture of her, to stress her character so well known ' and to appeal to them to concentrate only on the charge alleged. It was also brought out that she was often offensive to the guards and about the public and lawyers. Further that she could not find a gynaecologist to give evidence for her.

The first charge was not tried because of the magnitude of the second.

Nurse Cadden lived two floors up at 17 Hume Street and early in the morning of April 18, 1956 a woman's body was found on the pavement outside Number 15, two doors away. Naturally Nurse Cadden was suspected but a widespread police search was made of Number 17. The State Pathologist, Dr. Maurice Hickey, told the court that the woman was about thirty, was about five months pregnant and had had an abortion. An instrument had been inserted to pump in liquid or gas and death was caused by an air embolism which would cause death within two minutes. The woman's identity was soon found. She was Irish, married but living apart and had come to Dublin about a fortnight before.

Nurse Cadden denied to the police any knowledge of the matter. The gardaí found – openly – in her room two syringes, a forceps, two . – specula (instruments for examination of the womb), two pieces of rubber tubing, two very strong lamps and some rubber sheets. She said that she was now a midwife and had brought these things from her old nursing home. Asked about the syringes, forceps and rubber she said the former two were for midwifery and the rubber was for air. There were tiny specks of blood on the forceps and on the floor.

Asked to account for her movements on the evening of April 17th she gave an account of a visit from an old male client, whom she refused to identify. It was noticeable from her diary that all her other patients were female.

Mrs Farrelly from Number 15 and Mr. Kirwan from Number 17 were wakened during the night by dragging noises, in the former case for an hour and a half.

Nurse Cadden said she heard no noise such as Mrs Farrelly heard, perhaps because she had the radio on all night as she could not sleep; not what she had told Mrs Farrelly, that she was fast asleep. As to what Mr. Kirwan said she would not say.

At the trial, for the first time, a milk roundsman who discovered the body, said that when he was passing the end of Hume Street he saw a woman crouched on the footpath where he later found the body and saw her again in the basement of Number 15. His evidence was strongly challenged.

105

Dr. Hickey was in the witness-box for two days but maintained his original report.

At the end of the prosecution case the defence applied to have the case withdrawn from the jury for lack of evidence but the judge refused the application.

The defence did not call Nurse Cadden, but a few minor witnesses and Mr. Stanley her solicitor, who said that he had approached several gynaecologists (a) to advise the defence and (b) to give evidence, but none would agree to be 'mixed up' in the matter.

The jury were out for only an hour and found Nurse Cadden 'guilty of murder.' Asked if she wanted to say anything, she said, 'This is not my country. I am reporting this to the President of my country. This is the third time I am convicted in this country falsely. And I will report it, and I will see about it at a later date. Thank you. Only for my counsel I would say something you would not like to hear.'

The judge then sentenced her to be hanged and when he had finished spoke out again – 'Well, I am not a Catholic. Take that now.'

She appealed but was unsuccessful.

She was reprieved (no woman had been hanged in Ireland for over thirty years). The sentence was commuted to life imprisonment on January 4th 1957. Twenty months later she was transferred to the Central Mental Hospital at Dundrum and there she died suddenly eight months later, on April 20th 1959.

Legal Suggestions

There is nobody like a retired lawyer to make suggestions about 'legal reforms.' Out of many I pick the following:

JUDICIAL POSTSCRIPTS IN CRIMINAL CASES

It must surely be wrong for judges to say when a jury bring in a verdict of Guilty. 'I thoroughly agree with your verdict' or 'No other verdict was possible' or words to similar effect. That, with respect, is not his business and it casts serious doubt on the fairness of the Summing Up which preceded it. Also it usurps the function of the Court of Appeal, Criminal Division. In many cases over the past few years a judge has said words to that effect and the conviction has been quashed. A judge could give suitable punishment if he wishes without any reference to agreement or otherwise with the verdict of the jury. An example which occurs to me is 'The jury have found you guilty – stressing the word jury – of this very serious crime and it is now my duty to reflect their verdict in the sentence I now pass, which is X years imprisonment.'

'UNSAFE AND UNSATISFACTORY'

If I were completely innocent of a crime I would resent it deeply if my appeal were allowed on the statutory grounds of the charges having been 'unsafe and unsatisfactory' – as if it were only good luck which got me off, instead of being pronounced innocent. Why cannot we advise some other phrases, including the words 'wrong' or 'improper', to cover cases of where one is in fact innocent and should never have been convicted.

Why?

Why should the trial judge in a criminal case have (a) the prisoner's record (if any) before him throughout a trial, (b) the depositions (in Ireland – the Book of Evidence) before him all the time? I see no advantage in either and no consequence but possible prejudice to the accused. What is the point in the judge having the record? The fiction is – and it is pure fiction – that it is to help the accused and his counsel 'letting in the Record' by maladroit questions! What an extremely remote possibility. Much more realistic is that it will stay in the judge's mind, colour his approach to the case and interfere with a fair Summing Up. Judges can be as incapable as juries of 'putting things out of their mind' which they have seen or read. Why should the judge have the depositions? It is said that it is for him to prepare himself for objections or for him to note items which he might have to make out himself. All no doubt on the fiction of protecting the accused.

But why cannot a judge – like the jury – hear the case as it develops? Why should he have an advance copy of all the evidence given when the prisoner was committed? It can only lead to prejudice against the accused, by bungling prosecution witnesses up to proof. What point is there in a judge having all the known facts about the case in advance of trial and throughout trial – when the 12 true triers of the case have not?

Trust

I go aboard the aircraft
All ready to be flown,
By men I've never seen at all,
By men I've never known.

When I am safely seated
An anonymous voice comes through
To wish us all a pleasant flight
And introduce the crew.

This is the height of confidence
Placed in the great unknown –
Oh would we could trust others
As we trust pilots when we're flown.

Wigs, Bands and Robes

When the joy of the new robes has passed away there are some at the English and Irish Bars who agitate for the abolition of Wigs (principally), bands and even gowns for judges and Bar.

I do not see their objection. We have had them for over 300 years. They are a mark of dignity and superiority within the law and they clothe the man beneath whose words and advice would otherwise mean little.

In countries which have become independent of England many put at the foremost of their attacks the legal robes, but quite soon they go back to them. On the old Munster Circuit they abolished them after Independence for six months, but brought them back there on the footing that work had fallen off.

I think the public in general like them – as they like the judge to be all alone on a dais above them and they expect him to enter Court by a separate door.

When Ireland obtained Independence, all High Court and Circuit Court judges dressed in black gowns, and they still do. The Irish like pageantry and there is nothing more impressing (or frightening) than the Red Judge in England trying crime. I think it is a pity that the colour has gone out of Irish robes.

Another answer to the critics is that wigs, bands and robes are a uniform – a uniform of distinction.

Just like –

Crown and Peers' formal dress

Clerical dress (Catholic and Protestant)

Military dress (varying with rank plus ceremonial dress)

Naval and RAF dress (all countries and differing)

University dress (mortar boards, gowns and ribbons)

Teachers' dress (gown)

Top hat and tails

Police Force uniforms (varying with rank)

Fire Service uniforms

Railway official

Nurses (with differing colours, belts and bands)

Porters

Postmen

And scores of officials throughout public life.

It is not said of them that they are effete and old-fashioned. They do not wear their clothes for identity only but as a mark of dignity and respect for office.

If you would strip judge and Bar of their mark of office what would you do about the others I have named? Why not abolish the mitre, the crosier and the vestments? Why not put the Army in mufti? Or the police in shorts?

The robes are of English origin. In other countries they have different legal uniforms – Scotland (more dazzling than the English). France (gowns and special berets), the United States (gowns). Even in England the highest courts of all, the House of Lords and the Privy Council, sit in mufti. It is perhaps because of that one young Junior asked a senior colleague how to address them and was told 'Address them as if they were a Common Jury.'

I see no difference in the wig supplementing the berets or the headgear of other countries. It is striking that nearly all wear a gown instead of or as well as headgear. I believe that some headgear is needed – and why not a wig?

When Judges are wrong

Even judges are wrong – sometimes! But when they are what happens? Invariably the unsuccessful respondent in the Court of Appeal is ordered to pay the costs there and below.

Is this fair? After all the error was the judge's. He misinterpreted a document or a Statute, he followed the wrong fine of authority, he misinterpreted the cases he referred to.

Assuming a litigant who did not contribute to the judge's fault have to pay costs? In the Court of Appeal why should he have to do so – even if he seems to support the fault; after all he has a judgment for him, it has been laid down by the lawgiver and it is not the litigant's fault, but the judge's, which has led to the Appeal.

I would suggest a Special Fund out of which the costs of any sanctions could be paid. Without such fund the system is unfair.

Are Sanctions of Any Use?

Sanctions is a very impressive sounding word. It conjures up the picture of starving the victims step by step to abject surrender. SANCTIONS IMPOSED say the newspapers, proclaiming a case of death knell.

In the period during the Sanctions on Rhodesia I had a case before the Wells Street Magistrates in London, prosecuted by the late Sir Joseph Molony Q.C. (son of one of the last Chief Justices of Ireland in the old days).

My clients were charged with breaking the Sanctions by importing half a million pounds worth of machinery into Rhodesia and we (rather proudly) admitted the offence and pleaded guilty.

Saint Joseph (as I always mistakenly called him) looked as grim as ever when prosecuting, showing all the worry of the State at being outraged in this way.

The Magistrates (two men and a woman) looked at me as if I were a party to treason.

The Prosecution called a gentleman who was one of the people in charge of Sanctions and spoke of the very grave seriousness of the offence. He had the excellent habit for such a witness of clearing his eyes periodically, as if to dwell privately on the appallingness of the crime.

Very well briefed by our solicitor, I got up to cross examine.

'Does hardly anything get into Rhodesia from this country?' I asked.

'Hardly anything', he replied, with a good deal of pride.

'Look please at yesterday's copy of this Rhodesian paper, page 5.' Copies were handed in to the Magistrates.

'Does that page contain photographs of ten new British cars with price attached, available from a company at Salisbury?'

'It appears to.'

'Now please look at page 12. Does that show dresses 'Fresh from England'?

'They may not be from England.'

'Look again. Underneath three of them are where they're from.'

'Yes, I see.'

'Now please look at the Entertainments Page, page 30. Does that show three famous British actors and a British artiste appearing all this week and next at two theatres in Salisbury?'

'That's what it says.'

'Kindly put away that paper and take this one, an evening paper of the day before. Please turn to page 22. Does that show photographs of 12 gardening machines with British names and their price?'

'Yes.'

'Please turn to page 9 – does that show a photograph of stables being built by British Contractors?' 'It shows their name.'

'Do you doubt it?'

'I can't.'

'Finally would you look at page 1? Does that show a picture of both petrol and oil, make marked up, being poured into Rhodesia?'

'It could be anywhere.'

'Maybe you're right, but do you see below it two Rhodesian garages saying respectively 'Any Amount of Petrol' and 'Unlimited Petrol'?'

'Yes'.

I addressed three rather mystified Magistrates and called these sanctions a farce.

They withdrew in order to consider the fine and were out for about a quarter of an hour. The chairman made no comment at all but simply said 'Fined £10,000 and costs.' On machinery worth three quarters of a million it was distinctly good. It would obviously have been much more but for my solicitor's genius in conceiving the idea of the advertisements and producing them.

I had two other cases of sanction-breaking in respect of South African Sanctions and though not able to produce papers (I think they were burned!) I was able to use much the same technique in both, largely through getting to know from books the commodities South Africa would stand in need of and then using detailed knowledge about aircraft, cars, agricultural machinery and railways when in questioning the Prosecution's main witness as to whether they were still running, where did they get their petrol and oil, their spare parts and their repairs. He invariably did not know and I was able to point out that this was most surprising from one of the top people in Sanctions. In one case we were fined (again) £10,000 and costs for something like half a million pounds worth of French wine and in the other £5,000 for abut the same amount of tyres.

These few cases convinced me that all sanctions anywhere were only of limited worth in the modern world. Because there are so many sources of supply and because the consigning to a friendly country from England can easily and quickly end up in the Sanctioned territory. Moreover, the Sanctioned territory is often on the sea, or has friendly neighbours by the sea, and the vastness of the sea can conceal much. Armed blockade is plainly a very different matter.

An Interim Court of Appeal?

A large number of criminal and civil cases last two, three months and even more. In most points of law occur during the case and are ruled upon by the judge.

But what happens if the judge is wrong? – if the case proceeds in accordance with his ruling? It must go on to the end and then go in the ordinary way to the Criminal or Civil Court of Appeal.

It is to that situation that I make my suggestion that we should have an Interim Court of Appeal to decide the question in mid-trial and thus prevent the case going off on the wrong lines or dismiss the objection and uphold the judge.

This could save a lot of time and a good deal of money. Because its finding could not be disturbed later (save by the House of Lords).

It would, I suggest, need the leave of the trial judge or of the Interim (Special Court of Appeal) for a point or points to be argued before them. Meantime the trial would be adjourned pending their ruling. It should not take long, because the work-load, though important, would not be great.

If you think of any long case you will see that the judge has to rule many times, and what he rules often directs the whole future of the case.

Smuggling

In his retirement Vice-Admiral Sir Horace Paddington used to make fortnightly trips from Heathrow to France.

He was a tall and large man, and for his trips he wore full morning dress and a tall top-hat for his capacious head.

As well as Duty Free, which he carried openly, he bad for some three years packed his enlarged trouser pockets and the space under his hat with all sorts of dutiable goods – on many of which he made a handsome profit.

He was known to the Customs and Excise men as 'The Nibs' or 'The Old Geezer.' They never stopped him, because he looked the picture of utter rectitude.

Then one afternoon coming back from France two customs officers stopped him. He glared and looked as if his virtue had been suddenly violated – as indeed it was.

'Would you kindly take off your top-hat, sir?'

'Most certainly not.'

'And turn out your trousers, please', said the other Officer.

'I most definitely won't.'

The questions and the requests were repeated.

'Very well, sir, we will have to search you. Will you please go into that room over there?' 'How dare you', he said.

'Come along now or we'll have to drag you in.'

'It's absolutely monstrous.'

They manoeuvred him in. 'Take off that hat.'

Clutching it firmly he said 'I will not.'

'What is under it?'

'My hair, you bloody fool.'

'We're going to prise it off your head.'

'Just try.' They sent for two other officers.

The four men after a good struggle got the hat off.

There was absolutely nothing there – except the wisps of white hair.

Rather mollified the Chief Officer asked him to be good enough to turn out his trousers.

'No – you'll have to force me again.'

One Officer took one pocket, another took the opposite one. A third took the back pocket.

Nothing there except a few items and his Boarding Pass. They then searched his coat and waistcoat.

Completely empty. With apologies they released him.

On the next two trips he smuggled nothing but then resumed the hat-trick and the trouser-trick.

It continued for the next three years – undisturbed.

Then, when he was getting too old to do the French trip

regularly, his wife told him how much she missed the jewellery and expensive perfumes. She asked him how he did it.

'Quite easy', he said. 'I'd been doing it for some time and feared eventual detection. So one day I wrote an anonymous letter to the Chief Customs Officer at Heathrow and told him that an eccentric individual with a top hat and roomy trousers was regularly smuggling contraband under his hat and in his trousers. He told his men to look out for me. I carried nothing but made a hell of a row. I was never stopped again.'

The exalted smuggler then chose one of his special French Cigars and lit it with one of his gold Parisian fighters, 'I believe', he said, 'in a wider and commoner market.'

Ties

I was before my fellow countryman Judge McCreary (graduate of Trinity College, Dublin – T.C.D.) at Swindon on a Factory Act accident case. I was for the plaintiff and it was a 50-50 case. My efforts to settle it were all rebuffed. So we went into Court.

When my plaintiff was giving evidence the judge gave him some pretty hard digs, but I was accustomed to that and knew that if so he could dig deeper and better with the other side. The only trouble was that with so evenly balanced a case one did not want anything irrevocable said against the client.

Medical reports were not agreed so I called as my next witness our Consultant. As he was recounting his diagnosis and qualifications I noted with joy that he was wearing a T.C.D. tie. There was no mention at all of T.C.D. but he was greeted with great courtesy.

When he was being cross examined on the rival doctor's report the judge became irritable and then hostile.

My client had amongst other things fractured both hands. When they came to that the judge said to my opponent 'Has your expert ever operated on hands?'

After taking instructions my colleague said, 'No, but he has had considerable experience of damaged hands.'

'You heard what the Plaintiff's doctor said – that he had performed countless operations on both hands.' I sniffed to myself at the idea of a left hand only surgeon.

'Go on with the hands if you want to.'

The whole of the other side were harried. Their unfortunate doctor had his degrees and experience contrasted unfavourably with that of the T.C.D. expert.

'Have you written any learned papers?' asked the judge.

The witness thought for a moment and replied, 'Yes, the importance of the Mouth.'

'I don't want Student Theses. Give me something original.' The poor doctor forgot what he had even written.

The factory manager and the factory owner got hell. The judge seemed to be suggesting that it was a makeshift factory, every part of which was a hidden danger.

I will not say that T.C.D. turned the balance but it was no hindrance. Our evidence was better. The plaintiff won and got £11,000 plus his Special Damages and costs. About £2,000 more than he was strictly entitled to.

I saw the T.C.D. doctor in the car park later. I congratulated him on his evidence and asked him if he was Irish.

'Good Heavens no', he said, 'A Londoner born and bred. Why do you ask?'

'Well you're wearing a Trinity College, Dublin, tie.'

He laughed, lowered his voice to a whisper and said, 'I have a load of university, regimental and club ties in the back of the car plus a couple of reference books. When I find out what judge I'm appearing before, I look him up and then wear a tie according to his colours.'

'Where were you educated?' I asked.

'Princeton, U.S.A.' he said.

Stories

A French policeman gave a driver a breathalyser test. He then pronounced the result. 'Yes', he said, 'Chateau Lafitte 1951 – not a good year but not without breeding.'

* * * *

A man went to confession but unfortunately to a very deaf priest. 'I've killed my wife, father.'

'Speak up I can't hear you.' This went on two or three times and then the priest said he could hear.

'Ah yes', he said, 'How many times my son?'

* * * *

'I've taken counsel's opinion about your cases', said the solicitor, to his two clients.

'And what did he say?'

'He said you should escape immediately.'

* * * *

Counsel asked the witness in cross-examination, 'Isn't that witness a relative of yours?'

'Yes', said the Irish witness, 'by bigamy.'

* * * *

A lay friend was quizzing his barrister friend at their club. 'Just think you'd defend any old drunken rogue just for money.'

'Oh Fred', said the barrister, 'What have you been up to now?'

* * * *

At the end of a long civil case a woman juror got up and asked if she might ask a question.

'Certainly', said the judge, 'if it's relevant.'

'What', she said 'does plaintiff mean and what does defendant mean?'

* * * *

Scotland Yard were looking for a man. They circulated the police stations with four photographs of the man from different angles. Next morning they got from Cork this message, 'Have arrested three of the men. Hopeful of getting the fourth tonight.'

* * * *

In Ennis, County Clare, an accused man had an alibi. After four hours the jury came back.

The foreman said, 'We find the offence strongly proved.'

'Well that's that', said the judge, 'Guilty.'

'Well I don't know', said the foreman. 'We're not satisfied it was the Accused.'

* * * *

'Your counsel has kept telling me that you're a Jekyll and Hyde character. All right, let both of you go to jail for five years.

* * * *

'I leave myself in your Lordship's arms with great confidence', said a young barrister. 'With the same confidence that you've shown, Mr Jones?',' asked the kindly judge.

* * * *

It was outside Mr Justice Daly's Court in Dublin that a wife asked her barrister husband was it not prejudicial to have an accused in the dock, where he could readily be recognised. 'Why not a chair outside the dock?'

'Come in and hear this judge, darling. Then you'll see that there would be a grave danger in your suggestion of the prisoner leaping up and beating the living daylights out of him.'

Payments into Court

The Rule in England and Ireland is that in a civil claim a defendant can pay into Court a sum of money, which the plaintiff can take out in settlement. If he receives the amount in Court or less the regular rule is that he has to pay both sides' costs.

I find this completely unjust and that costs should be left to the discretion of the judge.

I have had (as I remember) two such cases. One was a personal injuries claim where my plaintiff got exactly what had been paid into Court. In spite of my speech where I said that the scheme was iniquitous that it was all guesswork by the judge – and who sustained the injuries, my client or the other side's insurers? He was ordered to pay both sides' costs.

The other case was one of prolonged and damaging nuisance. All damages awarded were something like £10,000 and there was £4,000 more in Court. It was purely a case of judicial guesswork and my client had to pay everyone's costs.

Why should it not be left to the civil judge to weigh everything up – including the payment in and all the difficulties of the case – and make such order as is just.

I knew a couple of judges who mischievously got around the Rule by asking counsel for the plaintiff to quantify all special damages and general damage.

A Jury

It was a murder trial where I was the judge at the Old Bailey. The accused was a young man of twenty charged with murdering a complete stranger by several knife wounds when going up and down a street mugging people on a Saturday night with three others. All in a highly populated London suburb.

The police were pretty sure that they had got the right men. Two passers-by identified him from each side of the road. He did not disappear with the others but ran a few yards away and the

119

police found the knife in a hedge. They found four similar knives in his bedroom at home but no weapons in the other young mens' homes. None of them would say anything. I had to stress very carefully to the jury about the identification evidence; that it had to be looked at very closely because there had often been honest but wary misdirection in the Courts. They must weigh it up with the other evidence. Rather to my surprise the defence called the accused. He had no Record (what about all the knives, I thought, knives with special pointed ends?). He was a good witness. When asked in cross-examination Who did it? he declined to answer directly, just said, 'I know who dun it and it wasn't me. I'd be murdered if I said.'

Asked about all the knives he said, 'I collect 'em. No 'arm in that.'

'What do you use them for?'

'I make models.' His solicitor later collected a few and brought them to Court. They were certainly very good.

I sent the jury (nine men, two women) out at 11 a.m. and went on with another case. They had lunch in their room. At 3 p.m. I brought them back and gave a majority verdict direction but stressing the desirability of a unanimous verdict.

Four times then before 6 p.m. they came back to ask questions – all relevant. Each time I asked them whether I could assist them further in their deliberations and each time the foreman said No. They had dinner in their room.

At 9 p.m. I asked them if they thought it likely they could agree upon a verdict. Without any qualification the foreman said Yes.

I had never before met this at the Bar or on the Bench. The nearest I had come to it was in a capital case of murder when I was defending, the jury were out for just over 12 hours and then brought in a unanimous verdict of guilty. But that was a case of capital murder. I was careful not to impose time-limits on the jury, because I remembered the case of a senior judge who had done it because he wanted to go to a Cattle Show Dinner in London and found the Court of Criminal Appeal very critical when setting aside the verdict of guilty.

I asked for counsel to come in to see my in my room. I said,

'What puzzles me most is their refusal to ask for any further assistance. What is your view?'

Both counsel said they had never come across anything like it but both said they wanted it to go on.

'Alright,' I said, 'I'll let it run into tomorrow but if their attitude is the same later tomorrow I'll discharge them and order a new trial.'

'With respect can you do that?', asked prosecuting counsel, 'if they say they want no further help.'

'But there must come a time when I can interfere.'

'I see what my friend means', said defending counsel. 'The accused is in the hands of the jury'.

I arranged for beds at a nearby hotel and a meal for the jury and adjourned to the next day at 10.30 a.m.

At 3 p.m. I sent for the jury, 'Is there any hope of your reaching a verdict?'

'Yes,' said the foreman.

'Can I help you in any way?'

'No, thank you My Lord.'

At 4.30 p.m. I did the same again. Precisely the same wordings and the same reply.

At 5.30 p.m. I did the same again. The same replies. I then said, 'Members of the jury you have obviously taken great care about this matter but I have come to the conclusion that it would be unfair to the Crown and the defence to let you go on deliberating. Despite what has been said I think there is no prospect of an agreement and I propose to discharge you and order that the prisoner be remanded for a new trial before another judge and jury.'

There was no commotion from anybody. There was no appeal.

About a month later I met the judge who had taken over.

'What happened?'

'Guilty,' he said. 'Jury out less than half an hour, unanimous.'

He then went on to tell me that at the end he had congratulated the chief inspector. 'I said to him I expect you have a lot of trouble with this sort of thing at weekends.' And he replied, 'Not only at weekends, My Lord, pretty well every single night.'

Forfeiture

Dangerous driving, excessive speed, cutting in and drunken driving are every-day events on our roads, Irish or English. A surprising number escape. But there are several deaths and serious injuries involved.

The conventional penalties are all right – so far as they go; except I would recommend that disqualifications should not be lifted before the date fixed by the Trial Court. I have heard accused say at times that they will not drive again yet apply – successfully – for removal of the disqualification after only half the period has run.

I believe in hitting the guilty where it hurts. On and after a second offence for the above let a man or woman be liable to permanent forfeiture of the car or motor bicycle. If there is hire purchase owing let it continue. If the car or motor bicycle belongs to somebody else, let it be capable of forfeiture and leave the parties to work out their own rights.

I believe that forfeiture of valuable possessions would be an additional safeguard in other crimes as well.

'I'm sorry, but while you were out shopping your daughter divorced you and the judge gave her the house, the car and the custody of the dog . . . '

Question Paper for very Advanced Students

Honours School of Jurisprudence

Because of my academic record – M.A. (Oxon) etc., always include etc. – I have been chosen by The Open and Shut University to set and correct their paper for the Finals of their Honours School of Jurisprudence. Here is my first draft:

1. Was it treason to execute Charles The First? If so, who was liable?

2. Today many people get out of 'The Tower' voluntarily. Name six who got out there involuntarily.

3. In a crowd you speak of your doctor as being 'an unqualified success'. Is this defamatory?

4. In a tennis tournament a young lady in temper strikes a ball, hits the umpire on his ladder and knocks him to the ground. He suffers multiple injuries and is confined in Wimbledon Hospital for eight weeks and is fearful of umpiring tennis again. Discuss liability. Would your answer be the same if the shot took place in a friendly?

5. How would you run with the reversion?

6. Who first said 'Res ipse Loquitor'? And why?

7. How many Law Lords sat on the celebrated case of *Donoghue v Stevenson*?

8. You are playing the 18th hole at golf and by reason of a mis-hit you break a window of the club bar and your ball hits and kills a man mid-Guinness. Discuss liability. Would your answer be the same if (a) he never golfed but drank, (b) he had just golfed, (c) he was about to golf?

9, You are a plutocrat and own a castle. On going away for three months you instruct Messrs Spade to demolish the East Wing. On your return you find the whole castle demolished. They say that it demolished itself through each piece crumbling in front of them as they hacked and they had to go on to avoid public danger. Advise. If you were tenant of the castle under a full repairing covenant what would the position be?

10. Distinguish 'No case to answer' from 'No answer to the case'.

11. To protect your neighbour's sheep from a fox you take out a gun. The fox escapes but you kill four of your neighbour's sheep. Analyse carefully.

12. How many of Lord Denning's judgments were approved by the House of Lords?

13. What is Volanti not a defence to?

Jennifer, the ex J.P. answers your questions

(No responsibility is accepted by authoress or publishers)

Jacqueline (Galway) — 'Clerical error' no longer means what you say. It has a distinctly wider meaning now.

Michael (Bath) — This is what is called an Inland Revenue demand. No, I can't say how they got you, but see an accountant immediately.

George (Durham) — This is a High Court writ, making a claim on you. You had better go to a solicitor today – as I have had the Writ for over four months. See conditions as to no responsibility above.

Maeve (Meath) — When you ordered a new refrigerator you had a right to a white one, not a red one. You don't say how long you have had it; undue delay might harm your claim. Write to the distributors.

Barry (Glamorgan) — £200 for 'thinking about your case' seems very steep in your Solicitor's Bill. Write to the ombudsman or see a 'Taxing Master' at the Law Courts.

Drug-taker (Woking) — No. Both morphine and arsenic are hard drugs. Your friend is wrong.

124

W. (Fermanagh)	To say to you 'The first Mrs W. (your mother-in-law) was a lady' is not defamatory, because it was spoken to you only.
Blanco (Isle of Man)	These two words are now a constant part of the English language and mean nothing actionable.
Foxy (Cornwall)	You called your doctor 'my old quack' in company. He is threatening to sue you. Please write again and say whether he is a specialist or a GP. It might make a difference. How old is he?
Paddy (Donegal)	You ask what are 'The Ends of Justice'. The answer is a final appeal.
Writer (Mayo)	How, you ask, would you address your successful leading counsel. I would suggest 'Counsel of Perfection'.
Stamp (Wexford)	'The Last Post' depends on the context in which it is used. Final musical farewell, last post collection, mile post.
All In (Darlington)	'A Refresher' means a daily recurrent fee to a barrister. An 'All In' fee is a once and for all fee, if agreed. It really comes to a bet on both sides as to how long the case will last.
Enquirer (Tipperary)	You cannot marry your grandmother. No – not even in the Cayman Islands.
Judge (Dublin)	It could be nerves or the onset of senility. See a doctor.
Doubtful (Barry)	No, certainly not. Criminal and immoral.
KN (Derry)	The next of kin count for nothing if there is a valid Will leaving them nothing. It's just family feuding carried on to the end.
Secundus (Tyrone)	'A second opinion' means the taking of a

	second doctor's opinion. It also applies to lawyers.
Bow (Waterford)	You win the bet. Bow Street is in London, Bow Lane is the Distillery HQ in Dublin.
Bookie (Kilkenny)	'First past the post' is a pretty unfair rule. A punter should be allowed to back the winner.
Teacher (London)	No – you mustn't throw pellets at pupils even in revenge.
Young Solicitor (Dublin)	Heading letters to a girl 'Without Prejudice' gives you no legal protection.
Practitioner (Co. Down)	Naming a horse after your unfavourite judge can be dangerous or helpful. It depends on how you phrase it.
Senior Partner (Leeds)	Acknowledging a letter by a blank sheet of paper (save for your address) may be anything you mention but can lead to trouble.
Hen House (Nervous)	You propose to turn an old existing toolshed into a hen house. I don't think this needs planning permission.
Patrick (Clare)	I'm afraid Gin is an intoxicant.

Proof Positive

What do you do in a criminal case if your client, the accused, suddenly departs entirely from his proof of evidence and from all that he has told you in a series of consultations?

It happened to me once, and once is quite enough.

I had a twelve-page proof of evidence of the client admirably prepared by my instructing solicitor in this case of massive fraud.

126

The proof said firstly that he had never met Mr John Smith, a material member of the coterie, who had disappeared.

'Did you ever meet Mr John Smith?', I asked.

To my astonishment – which had to be hidden – he said, Yes, several times.'

What could be asked next? One couldn't ask him, without misleading the Court, when did you first meet him? Or anything in that vein, so I settled rapidly for, 'And then?'

Fortunately he followed it up for some twenty minutes on meetings with Mr Smith, I prompting him – in similar fashion – from time to time.

But I was placed in great difficulty about his twelve-page Proof of Evidence. Everybody – judge, jury, opponent – would expect me to turn over each page as I got to the end of it.

But that would be calculated deception.

I had some time to think on this occasion and decided, as unostentatiously as I could, to put my brief on one side and concentrate on the accused.

At long last Mr John Smith finished and we had about a quarter of an hour 'right up to proof'.

The next part of the proof dealt with two financiers he had met for three long interviews at the Midland Hotel, Manchester. They were not – yet – in the dock. In his proof he put a large part of the blame on them.

I was by now so chary of the client that I did not give him a clue word such as Manchester to lead him on to the next header.

'Do you know a Mr George Shot?'

'No,' he said.

'Or a Mr Henry Blunt?'

'No,' he said.

With those two answers four pages of his interviews with them collapsed.

I had to remember where we had got to. Ah yes – plain sailing for a few minutes.

Then finally his proof spoke of two visits to Bristol where the prosecution said the plot was finally hatched. His proof dealt fully with his two visits to Bristol, how convenient they were and exactly what he had done.

It was safe enough to ask him if he had ever been to Bristol.

Rubbing out the last three pages of his proof he said, 'No.'

'That, My Lord,' I said with great relief, 'is the end of my examination in chief.

The client was convicted and got seven years. Privately I hold the view that he thoroughly deserved it – for departing from his proof.

Over-Night

I had seen their advertisements – Fly Your Furniture Over-Night England – Ireland. I remember wondering how they would get from Carlisle to Dingle over-night.

Then one afternoon I had a Consultation with a charming Irish lady of about 40, recently widowed, who had availed – or tried to avail – of that service.

She and her husband had a small flat in Chelsea for the purpose of his business. Their real home was a large Georgian residence in County Wicklow, where she spent most of her time. Now that her husband had died she was proposing to sell the Chelsea flat and move completely to County Wicklow. There were about twenty-five items of furniture, glass, silver, cutlery and ornaments which she wanted to bring with her. Then she saw this enticing advertisement and called into their office off the Strand. Cordially greeted all particulars were taken down and she – foolishly – parted with a cheque for £550.

Was the advertisement correct?, she asked. Absolutely – expect two men at your flat tomorrow and arrange for somebody to meet the furniture the day after.

What about Insurance? Not to worry, we take care of that.

She thought the price a bit steep, but then of course there was a lot of loading and unloading involved, and there was free Insurance.

Like so many other people she did not look at the back of the Invoice she received. She showed it to me and having read it I said, 'It excludes so much that I think a Court would hold that it excludes nothing.'

The company's men did not arrive next day, but three weeks later. The furniture and chattels did not arrive next day but nine months later (yes nine months). She had telephoned the company and written to them several times, but to no avail.

'It's intolerable,' I said, 'but what other loss can we prove apart from the £550 and the telephone calls and the postage?'

'What about worry and shock?', Asked the solicitor.

'They certainly should apply here but I'm afraid they don't. They're hard enough to prove even in an accident case.'

The client was despondent. I asked her, 'Would you have used any of those things during the nine months?'

'Probably, only the silver cutlery once or twice.'

Ending on an optimistic note I said, 'I think one way and another I can get you something a lot better than £550,' and I asked the solicitor to have a writ and statement of Claim prepared obtaining damages for breach of contract, negligence and deceit.

About a fortnight later I had a telephone call from my opponent. 'I'm in this Irish furniture case, my dear fellow.'

'Yes,' I said, 'you must settle it.'

'How much do you want?'

'£5,000 and indemnity costs.'

'What did you say?'

I repeated it.

'But my dear fellow you got the furniture. We were thinking of a token payment of £500.

'Far too token.'

'But remember we have all these conditions and exceptions.'

'You can forget them,' I said, 'not worth a match.'

'Well, he said, I'll have to get in touch with my people but it looks like a fight.'

'One last word, I said, 'It would be for me to open the case. And can your people imagine the headlines in the English and Irish papers next morning?'

A week later he called to see me and we settled for £4,000 and indemnity costs.

Stamping It Out

I defended a retired civil servant in his mid-sixties at the Old Bailey for stamp frauds.

He was a very respectable man with an excellent record. He was on bail and told us his story in Chambers.

I must be careful in telling the story because the trial judge had part of the evidence taken *in camera* 'in case other people hear about this'. It's a long time ago and the judge has long gone but the Post Office still exists.

The client said that he took the matter up 'as a hobby'! It started when he mistakenly posted two letters without any stamps and found that they arrived without any surcharge. They were the only 'successes' he had. The next six he did were all surcharged. The same happened when he put blank sticky labels on the envelope and when he put grossly inadequate stamps on letters.

He then turned to putting on foreign stamps; no good.

He next put inadequate stamps all over the envelope, back and front; hopeless.

He was finally caught when he forged and sent 'Free Post' envelopes. A watch was kept on him as he posted a number of them.

'It was fun,' he said, 'while it lasted.' None of us looked at it in quite that way.

'I didn't do it to defraud anybody,' he went on. 'It was really an experiment and it didn't come off.'

'How many phoney letters did you post, and over what period?', asked my junior.

'Perhaps a hundred. Over fifteen months or so. I didn't do it every day, you know.'

'Did you ever post any ordinary mail?', I asked.

'Oh yes,' he said, 'hundreds.'

After a lot of discussion we decided to plead Not Guilty, and when we felt we had established his good record and the amateur nature of the frauds, to change the plea to Guilty.

At the trial we had another high civil servant as a character witness.

I saw no less than four well-dressed men, obviously top

scientific officers of the Post Office, wondering no doubt why this was not a plea of Guilty.

The judge began by taking a serious view – and went on taking it.

I got out the accused's record easily enough. But I was not getting very far with the experts. When I asked one whether the total amount defrauded was probably less than £5 he answered disconcertingly, 'As far as we know.' When I asked another if the frauds weren't very amateur he said, 'Some were quite good.'

We decided to change our plea just after lunch. When I asked the judge if the client could have bail over lunch he said, 'No. Take him down, warders.'

After lunch we called the character witness, who was very good.

I mitigated for about half an hour without any interruption – stony silence.

When I had finished – listing my client's means as a last resort – we expected the judge to pass sentence. Instead he said, 'I take a very grave view of this case. A deliberate series of frauds on the public. I will postpone sentence until the day after tomorrow at 10.30. Remove him, warders.'

When we got out of Court my junior said, 'That means a fine.'

The solicitor and I were not so sure.

Two days later an ashen-faced, wobbly, client went into the dock. The judge watched closely for about two minutes and then said, 'You are a miserable, mischievous fraud. You deserve to go to prison, and you've seen what it's like. The sentence of the Court on all these charges is that you pay a fine of £4,000 and £1,000 costs within six months from today. One year's imprisonment in default.'

Noting Brief

There is a subtle distinction between A Noting Brief and – Watching Brief – the jealous prerogative of the young barrister. To put it briefly (a fateful beginning by many judges) A Watching Brief is to Watch (like a Lynx) all that is said and done in Court and to report to your Instructing solicitor each evening, whereas A Noting Brief is to take a Note (slavishly) of everything said in Court and to report the important parts that evening. As one of nature's worst notetakers (and not a great believer in them either) I much preferred the Watching Brief, but since both were equally miserably paid I would gladly accept either. One afternoon after about two years Call Clement came into my narrow little room and said 'Got you a good Noting Brief for Reading Assizes – 35 guineas a day – might last two weeks.' And he handed over a very thin Brief headed something like 'Re The British Aerospatical Corporation.' Thanking our splendid Clerk, who miraculously managed to keep all the young men busy, I sat down to read this magnificently marked Brief. I wondered how this world-famous Corporation could be interested in a criminal case. Perhaps an ex-employee I thought.

The Instructions were to this effect – 'Six months ago four men broke into the factory near Reading by levering open part of the roof. They escaped in the same way, taking over £7,000 of money and a number of valuable instruments and keys. They are being tried tomorrow and it is understood that all four are going to plead Not Guilty.'

So far so good. Then came the surprise, 'Our clients were the owners of these premises until two years ago, when they sold them to the present owners Reading Ready Reckoners. Our clients are naturally concerned that any suggestion might be made as to the inadequacy or lack of repair of the roofing. Counsel will please take a Note accordingly and kindly get in touch with Mr Blackhead, our senior partner, immediately after the visiting of the Court each day.' The senior partner! (I do not think I had ever met or spoken to a senior partner before) but then of course they were extremely important clients.

I wasn't too good on pure Law – I'm still not – but it struck me that the clients had nothing at all to worry about. They'd sold the building a long time ago, presumably there had been a full survey and nobody had blamed them in any way about the roofing.

I went upstairs to Clement and told him that I felt the clients need not be represented and that I proposed to ring up the solicitor accordingly. He greeted the news with the shock and annoyance of any first-rate barrister's clerk at work being 'thrown away'.

'Look J.C.,' he said, 'they know their own business. Say nothing and go there; and stay there – at 35 guineas a day – until they stop you.'

I went down the first day. Counsel in the Robing Room were very curious as to who – and what – I was. I said I had 'A Noting Brief' but declined to say who for. They were all very suspicious. The only references to 'our' roof were when prosecuting counsel said that entry had been gained by the roof and the managing director confirmed it. Not one word of criticism of 'our' roof.

I reported that evening to the Senior Partner, who said the clients would be delighted! Before I was able to voice any anti-Clement doubts about going on appearing he said 'The clients would, I know, wish you to stay to the very end. Just report to me if ever the roof is mentioned.'

For twelve solid days I went up and down to Reading, at a fee per day beyond my wildest dreams. I got friendly with the other counsel, who apparently decided that I must be representing an insurance company!

On about the eighth day the judge – an affable man – became interested in me and as he rose for lunch asked his clerk to enquire who I was and who I represented. I told the clerk but asked the clerk that the name of my clients should not go beyond the judge.

When the Court resumed at 2 o'clock the judge, smilingly, turned to me and said 'Mr Conningham, I understand you appear for an interested party?'

'Yes, My Lord.'

'I think it had better be recorded in the shorthand note from the beginning – for the sake of completeness. Would you, Mr Conningham, kindly hand in your name and that of your Instructing solicitors at your convenience to the Shorthand Writer? And, Miss Shorthand Writer you need only put down 'appeared for an interested party'. Mr Conningham gave me the name and I have noted it in my Book.' I felt a great glow of esteem at having been mentioned in Court – albeit under the wrong name.

All four men were found Guilty and the only other mention of the roofing came in the sentencing. The judge said 'This was a brazen. well thought out robbery, you four arming yourselves with a battery of tools to prise open this highly secured roof.' I wrote down and solemnly underlined these splendid words about the roof. I rang the solicitor from the railway station and he was delighted 'Well done, he said, I having of course done nothing. 'The clients will be relieved.' I still couldn't think why. 'Would you,' he went on, 'do a four or five page Note of the whole proceedings – for an extra fee of course – which the Chairman could lay before the board?' I said I would be delighted and did it that night.

This ends my mundanely extraordinary story of the Noting Brief – but there is a postscript. That six weeks later the same firm had another Noting Brief again in Reading. I could not do it and there was no young junior in chambers available. Clement 'passed it over' to friendly chambers next door – on the usual 'you remember me next time' basis.

They had a young man available and he took the Noting – or perhaps in the circumstances Watching – Brief.

For ten days at Reading he Noted or Watched so well that he fell for the Shorthand Writer in a big way, and she for him. They were soon married, and she had to keep him for some years until he got a practice.

For months in Chambers I had to assure my friends in Chambers that I had not either 'Noted' or 'Watched' her. My mind was up on the roof.

Knowing

I hope it does not sound arrogant but I regard it as a golden rule for barristers and solicitors in litigation to find out all they can about the judge, the other side, their witnesses and if possible the jury, before the case begins. I was always taught that by my father and uncle, but (like so much else) it does not impress itself on you until you experience it yourself. I was about ten years at the Bar when, fortuitously, this Irish lady, now living in London, was brought to me about maintenance from her ex-husband of forty years standing– The solicitors were comparatively new clients and did not know I was Irish. Nor did the client until we met.

The surname was an unusual one, not met much in England. They owed their prosperity to a famous high quality store in Dublin, at which I had often shopped and was now sold. They lived in a County about fifty miles from Dublin – a large ancient Georgian house, beautiful gardens and woodlands, with about 400 acres of land. They advertised it for visitors for nine months of the year. He had two pedigree cattle herds, which he showed with success.

He had taken up with another woman, very much younger, and that was the cause of the divorce.

He was very mean to his ex-wife and so far as she was concerned was prepared to lie.

I told her I had visited the estate (house and gardens) twice. She told me what he had received for the store at that time (six and a quarter million pounds now fifty years ago). She gave me the details which only a long-standing wife would know.

I asked the solicitors to get me the following – photographs from the brochure, an ordinance map (from the office in the Phoenix Park), the Irish equivalent of Who's Who and a list of the winning cattle from the Royal Dublin Society (the premier cattle show) for 12 years.

His affidavits of means were short, abrupt, and in several respects untrue – suppressive rather than expressive. I got leave to cross- examine him. By that time he knew I was very clearly connected with Ireland.

I asked him about English assets first. He had suppressed a few but the first thing I asked him which shook him was whether certain Shares were 'On the English Register or the Irish Register'. He had a good many on the English Register – which we got the registrar to freeze.

I then asked him about gardeners and indoor servants and how he got on with the Revenue about it. He had 'upped' the gardeners and servants and 'downed' the receipts; they were paid in cash and he pocketed a good proportion daily. When I asked him how much the collectors got he said, 'About £19 a week, each.' On his ex-wife's instructions I asked him if the rollectors were always his grandchildren; he answered sheepishly 'Sometimes.'

'And you pay them untaxed out of the collection?'

'Have to,' he said, 'only ready money available.'

'What about your safe?'

'What safe?'

'The one you keep at the back of the cellar?'

'Oh that one. It's a very small safe.'

'Large enough to hold £10,000 or more?'

'It could do.'

'Does it?'

'I couldn't rightly tell you.'

'Would you mind the registrar going over to inspect it?' He looked at the registrar with surprise and the registrar said, 'I'd very much enjoy it.'

I asked him about clubs he belonged to – a remarkable number. I knew them all and where they were situated. 'Why, for example, belong to the Kildare Street Club and the Stephen's Green Club – they're only a mile apart?'

'More than a mile,' he said.

'Come now,' I said, 'turn left for 50 yards from the Green, go down Dawson Street 250 yards, turn right and in a couple of minutes you are at the Kildare Street Club.'

Marvelling at one who knows Dublin so well, he simply said, 'Yes.'

I taxed him about the proceeds of the sale of the store. 'It is all very complicated. My Irish solicitor could help but he isn't here.'

'Could we have him here tomorrow?'

'Might be difficult for him.'

'Name a day after the weekend adjournment, convenient to the registrar. Alright?'

'Very well – alright.'

I then turned to cattle. To give him his due he did not go in for private companies; what he owned, he owned personally. He could not deny strong personal knowledge of both herds; he was on the council of both societies and an accredited judge for the others. All this he admitted.

I brought him slowly through his Dublin winnings for twelve years; the prices at which he had sold; the extremely impressive

136

record of both herds. The total value of them; the cost of keeping them,

'Will you be long more?' Asked the registrar before the midday adjournment.

'Oh yes, sir – probably the whole afternoon. I have racing to cover and several other subjects.'

After the adjournment my opponent came up to me and said, 'He's absolutely fed up with you, Jimmy. What'll you take?'

We kept the registrar waiting and bargained for about half an hour. Then we received a very handsome settlement for the ex-wife (£75,000 lump sum, a largish monthly payment and costs). She deserved it all; an ageing castaway.

Roundabout

I think it is a great pity that certain Criminal Courts (JP's Courts, Stipendiary Courts and certain Circuit Courts) are in one or two places all the time. They should move around like High Court judges.

My objections are in number:

(1) They get to know – and respect – 'regulars' in their court, such as police and store detectives. So much so that when a police officer resigns one often hears the Bench saying 'We will miss you Inspector. You have been a great help to us over the years. We wish you a happy retirement.' This of an inspector who has given evidence to them or him on countless occasions! Usually to deny the accused's version! What would people convicted on his evidence have to say? Just that to that Bench he has been infallible.

(2) The local Bench often knows – can't help knowing – local reputations and gossip; and must be influenced by it. I know that in origin they were intended to act on 'local knowledge' and even 'hearsay'; but in the modern world that day is long since gone. Indeed High Court judges in important cases warn juries to disregard what they have seen or heard.

(3) They know – well or slightly – too many who give evidence before them. For example doctors, dentists, solicitors, counsel,

professional people, social workers etc. It is inevitable that there are likes and dislikes. The same with regard to local trades-people, friends or acquaintances.

(4) Sometimes it is right for the Court to have 'a view' of the scene of something, *e.g.* an accident. But far better not to know it and have long-standing views about it, *e.g.* 'it is notoriously dangerous', 'cars always exceed the speed limit there' etc.

Stafford and Luvaglio

This was a sordid and unpleasant murder case from Newcastle-on-Tyne. The facts and contentions are so complex that I do not propose to go into them more than my story requires. The case achieved certain notoriety and reached the House of Lords.

The two men in their middle thirties were convicted of murdering a juke-box collector, associated with both of them, by jamming his Jaguar car, shooting him and leaving him dead in his car. They completely denied doing it and had an alibi, quite well attested. Sir David Napley, Luvaglio's solicitor, and Dr Camps, the well known pathologist, ardently felt all their lives that Luvaglio was wrongly convicted. Sir David briefed me to lead John Matthew (one of the country's best counsel and a noted, superbly fair) prosecutor for Luvaglio.

We appeared before the Court of Criminal Appeal with our co-accused (separately represented).

I deeply resented what the judge had said about Luvaglio in his Summing Up – that he said he was a friend of the deceased 'but remember Judas' and later 'the ides of March are upon us' (*i.e.* Brutus). The judge was a friend of mine but I felt bound to castigate him for (to me) these most appalling observations. Perhaps the sordid atmosphere of the whole case – with prostitutes, gambling on machines on a huge scale, thieving by collectors, tax evasion by owners – carried him away.

I was bold enough to say that these two passages alone were sufficient to quash Luvaglio's conviction. The Appeal Judges plainly did not like them but got a little tired of me reiterating them. Lord Justice Edmund Davies (later Lord Edmund Davies) murmured quickly 'We have your point, Mr Comyn. Very much so. But shall we look at the evidence and the rest of the Summing Up?'

We did, and while they considered the judge's observations, they said it was a matter for the jury, fully argued and dismissed the appeal. Exactly the same happened in the House of Lords. But with great respect I hold strongly my own view, that in a heavily contested murder trial, these observations vitiated the result.

Criminal Law Review – Some New Suggestions

Criminal law review is very much in the news. The current controversies are well known. There is, however, something which occurs to me as one who practised regularly in the criminal courts, which could be useful and should not be controversial.

I have long found beginnings of a criminal trial to have certain grave defects. First of all, the jury brought in to try the case (and it may well be their first experience of jury service) are given no kind of advance information as to the course the trial will take, apart from a little information as to hours of sitting, and so forth, on a short sheet of paper.

The first person they hear is the prosecuting counsel, who naturally goes straight into details of the case. It would, I think, be of enormous advantage if it became standard practice for the judge to introduce the case to the jury by telling them the nature of the charges, the procedure which would be adopted (*i.e.* opening speech, evidence, cross-examination, summing up), the hours the court would keep each day, how long they might be expected to have to stay on the case and what they would have to do at the end.

Taking up the latter point, it is surprising how many people serving on a jury for the first time think for a long period that they will be required to give a kind of detailed judgment rather like a High Court judge in a civil case. It may be many days before they realise that their total speech in the trial will be limited to either one or two words at the very end. It is also noteworthy that only on rare occasions are the jury supplied with what must be essential in every single case, ample room, foolscap pads and jotters and plenty of pens and pencils.

It is far too much to expect any juror to carry in his head for days important points which he has mentally noted in the course of the trial, and in that respect, he has been placed at a disadvantage which is not shared by the experienced lawyers in the case and the judge.

Leading on from what I have said above, I have also long considered that the prosecution have an undue advantage at the beginning of a criminal case. Prosecuting counsel opens it, without any real fear of interruption from the defence, and if the case is a long one, the opening could last as long as two or three days or more. And it is the prosecution opening which captures the headlines.

Following such opening, the prosecution call their evidence and if the first witness is a major one (as often happens) it may be days before the defence are heard at all. It would be much fairer if either of two new courses was adopted.

The first course is have the judge state the facts and issues and to confine the opening of a prosecution case to a bare outline of the basic matters – without comment; in other words, to alter its whole character from a speech to a statement.

The alternative course is, while preserving the right of the prosecution to a full opening speech, to allow the defence – at their option – to make a speech at the end of it and before any evidence is called. It is important that this should be optional and not compulsory, because there are, of course, many instances when the defence would find it embarrassing, or at any rate more likely to harm than to help.

The existence of such occasions, however, should not be allowed to obscure the importance of the defence being unable to say something at this stage if they want to.

The kind of case in which it would be of very great importance is where the defence want to make it clear that they are not disputing the basic facts but rather challenging some essential ingredient of the alleged offence, such as 'intention'. This would cover cases of killing where the defence intend to argue ultimately for a verdict of manslaughter rather than murder and it would also cover, of course, the numerous cases of stealing, forgery, fraud and so on, where 'intention' is all important. I have found it surprising (and when defending, often irksome) that it may be days before one can get over to the jury the important consideration that they need not worry themselves about some facts but should concentrate their attention either on other alleged facts or on inferences.

The instances which I have just mentioned are, of course, in no sense comprehensive and, on my suggestion, the defence should be given their right of early speech in any class of case and subject only to their choice to take the opportunity or to leave it.

There should be room in the re-shaping of our criminal law for some re-thinking upon these lines about the very beginning of a criminal case. The beginning is often a crucial stage It is sometimes too late to destroy first impressions days later.

Rustling

Up to 160 years ago stealing a sheep or animal was punishable by death. 'And quite right too,' the farmers would say, protesting at any reprieve. Cattle rustling still goes on in both England and Ireland. We had a period of it about ten years ago at Tara. Calves carried away in a largish trailer (with reversible number plates), from Dublin, Belfast etc. At dead of night they would carry away up to 10 calves – or a few cows or bullocks.

Locks did not deter them (wherever you situated them). They quickly hack-sawed them. I told the police next morning but they said there are so many licensed and unlicensed butchers throughout the country 'the beasts are cutlets now'.

I tried, with some success, putting three strings of the nearly permissible power electric fences at ten yard intervals. I had only one rustling after that. Indeed it has long since died down in Ireland. Although all sorts of cattle offences go unnecessarily on.

But two years ago a local farmer and friend rang me up to say that he had eight of his beautiful pedigree Devons stolen. When he went to the police they gave him precisely the same advice as my local police.

I told him about live electric wire advice and he tried it with success – but threading it through his gates. It worked.

But a month later they took his prize and rather docile bull.

He was not unnaturally near the house and in a stall of his own untethered.

He, like me and most other farmers, do not insure cattle because the premiums are high and to insure a whole flock or herd would be exorbitant.

I feel that cattle-stealing, rare though it is, should be severely punished. A city judge often does not appreciate what the farmer has lost; for example cows capable of producing several calves; a bull; or a bullock, part of a saleable herd.

As to cruelty to farm animals, I have only come across a very few in farming in the Law. Farmers are invariably very good about seeing to animals, well or ailing. The worst I ever came across was defending a Vet for gross cruelty (two animals dead, two dying and half a dozen half-starved). The explanation was not that he was a cruel man but 'was heavily on the bottle'. It needed some luck to keep him out of jail. The failure of neighbours to object was a helpful factor. He was fined £3,000 and was later struck off by his professional society.

Relieved

It was at a Magistrate's Court in, I think, Woking – at any rate a place run pleasantly and peacefully.

I was defending a man for receiving 12 rather valuable forks. The case against him was thin and at 45 years or so he had no previous convictions.

It was a warm and slumbering afternoon in mid-summer.

When the prosecution case ended I said, without turning round, 'The accused please.'

Nothing happened. A somnolent Bench woke up. A drowsy police officer in the dock shot up and said 'Christ, he's gone.'

A general hue and cry followed in Court and out of Court. Then suddenly the prisoner turned up and said to all and sundry

'That's better' – referring to the fact that he had just gone out to the lavatory.

A gentlemanly chairman said to him, 'You mustn't do that sort of thing. You're being tried.'

'You know what it is, sir. Caught short. Anyway I'm not convicted yet.'

Sternly I said 'Into the witness-box – nowhere else.'

He was acquitted. He said to me afterwards, 'Did I do wrong?'

I said, 'Yes you did – very wrong.'

'Well,' he said, 'I couldn't do justice to myself bursting as I was. My goodness didn't I feel better.'

The Letter

Lady Furnell had married great wealth, and apart from what was lovingly bestowed on her by her ever-loving she was possessed herself of extremely valuable jewellery, including the best gold ring Gerrards could supply.

One weekend she and her husband were going to a weekend party in Lancashire and sharing their compartment on the train were Mr and Mrs Smith, acquaintances of long standing. Lady Furnell was ostentatiously wearing (on two fingers) the best and most expensive of her rings.

Changing for dinner that evening Lady Furnell felt that it would look better if she discarded the wonderful rings and just wore her engagement and wedding rings.

To her consternation she found at dinner that the most valuable of all her rings she had left behind was reposing on Mrs Smith's finger.

She said nothing; nor on the next night, when the same thing happened.

When she got back to London – still minus her ring – she went to see her solicitor, Mr Cann.

'This needs to be handled tactfully,' he said, and thought about it for a few minutes.

Then he sent for the office boy and asked him to get a pre-paid registered envelope.

Meantime he started to draft a letter. In its final form it ran:

Dear Mrs Smith,

At the house party in Lancashire last weekend you obviously inadvertently took one of my client's rings and have so far not returned it. I enclose a pre-paid registered envelope for its return to me by the end of the week. If that is done it will be the end of the matter. Yours sincerely,

The office boy returned with the pre-paid registered envelope which Mr Cann addressed to himself. He then copied out the draft in his own handwriting, put the letter and the envelope in another, addressed to Mrs Smith and asked the office boy to register it.

Two days later, in the registered envelope supplied, the ring was returned – without any comment.

Sentencing

Periodically there is a public commotion about a sentence passed in court – as there recently was in England when an Old Bailey judge allowed a young double-rapist to retain his liberty.

It is right that the press and the public should be free to comment upon a judicial sentence, or indeed any judgment by a court of law. That the judge cannot in the nature of things reply is a necessary part of the legal system and no answer to the right of comment and criticism.

There are, however, certain important considerations which the public should have in mind when exercising their right. The first, and most important, is that in most cases only those engaged in or connected with the case or present in court during the whole of it can really know about it. And as a lawyer, I know only too well that even in a simple case, such as a plea of guilty to stealing, the lawyers in court and the spectators may all differ considerably between themselves as to the sentence give. Just as they so often differ about the result of a contested criminal case or civil action. There are undoubtedly many cases where the salient facts – on both sides – can sufficiently come across to the public to enable

144

them to judge, but in my experience that is the exception and not the rule.

The next point to appreciate is that the circumstances in a particular criminal case can differ greatly (a) from an apparently similar case and (b) between the various accused involved. For example what sounds terrible, or reads terribly, may have strong mitigating factors – such as provocation of a kind which is intense and prolonged but does not in fact amount to the legal defence of provocation. Again, as between various accused, there may well be very different degrees of blame and there will almost certainly be sharp differences in character, record and prospects. It may even be appropriate to make allowance for an accused having pleaded guilty – saving the victim of a sexual offence from having to give evidence or avoiding great expense and inconvenience to witnesses and others.

Two things which any experienced lawyer will confirm are – that a plea in mitigation is the hardest of all forensic tests and that it can make a very great difference. In spite of any amount of medical, probation, prison or social welfare reports a judge may derive the greatest assistance of all in sentencing from the counsel who mitigates for the accused. I certainly do not mean by that the familiar 'emotional' factors (a sick wife, five children, loss of a good job) but hitherto unrealised considerations which for example either explain why the offence was committed or what can be done for the offender and the public by way of rendering a return to crime unlikely.

Certain questions are often asked – Why leave it to one man to assess the sentence? Why is there no definite 'course on sentencing' for judges? Why is there no standard policy – a tariff – for sentencing? Why should there not be 'uniformity' between sentences? I will attempt to answer them and I believe there are ready, sensible, answers.

In England and Ireland most sentencing is in fact done by more than one man. Over ninety per cent of criminal cases in England and Wales are tried by lay magistrates. It is a staggering proportion but of course it includes such huge categories as traffic offences and does not include the more serious crimes. So far as lay magistrates are concerned, Ireland dispensed with them on inde-

145

pendence. So far as judges are concerned, it simply would not be practical to have as many as two or three to sit together for sentencing, and likewise the idea (often advanced) of having, say, a welfare worker and a psychiatrist to sit with the judge is not just or practical. Either proposal would be possible (however undesirable) in the case of a plea of guilty - but what about the long, maybe very long, contested case which results in a conviction? We cannot spare a number of judges to hear each contested case. We obviously cannot bring laymen into the trial of a case. And who but the judge who tries the case can properly sentence the convicted? Lest it be thought that I lay too much stress on long cases, it is important to realise that with the complexities of modern life the number of long criminal cases is increasing. In England ten or twelve week trials – and longer – are now commonplace. So far as pleas of guilty are concerned it would surely be illogical and quite wrong to have additional judges or the addition of laymen if that did not apply to contested cases. It would mean a two-tier or inconsistently-double system of criminal law.

As to the question about a 'sentencing course for judges', or (as I have heard it put) a 'degree in sentencing' the answer is two-fold: in England and Ireland there in fact are courses, in the shape of 'judicial get togethers' (they are dignified by the title of 'a symposium on sentencing'), and secondly judges have a long and wide experience, at the Bar and on the Bench – an experience which they lose no opportunity of increasing through study of medical and welfare views, visits to prison, comparisons with other lawyers and indeed in every way they can. More could probably be done in this situation.

There undoubtedly are bad sentences, just as there are bad judges, and good judges who have bad days. The pleasant fact is that these are the exceptions – very exceptional. The judge finds sentencing his most worrying task and he worries about it a lot. He has the independence, the detachment and the position which a layman cannot bring to the responsible job in hand. And he will tell you, I venture to think, that 'sentencing on paper' or in theory is vastly different from sentencing in practice. A regular example confronts him when he reads the papers in a criminal case in advance and may decide very provisionally the kind of sentence likely. When he hears the case 'live' his actual sentence will invariably be different – usually more lenient.

As to policy about sentencing – a tariff and/or uniformity – there is a broad policy: it can only be broad: there is, again in broad terms, a 'tariff': but with all of these there cannot be, and MUST NOT be, uniformity. The reason for that is because every case differs completely from another.

Bigamy

It was Lord Chief Justice Russell who said that the penalty for Bigamy is two mothers-in-law.

In the cases of the last two hundred years there are remarkably few of Bigamy. Many went unnoticed; others emerged in large cases, like The Brides in The Bath murder case – *R. v. Smith*, 1915.

It is surprising that the number of Bigamy cases remain constant today – with easier divorces, mutual unmarried cohabitation (which I think is potentially hard on the woman), the more open book of personal morals, the ease of foreign travel, the growth of population and the comparative ease of disappearance.

Why is Bigamy still committed? I believe there are main reasons:

(1) Pretence by man or woman that he/she is not married because the other would not live together otherwise.

(2) Pretence so as 'to bury the past'.

(3) Seduction.

(4) Singly or mutually to 'fool relations'.

(5) Singly or mutually to 'give a name' to a forthcoming baby.

(6) To get hold of the other's money.

(7) To facilitate some other crime less than murder.

(8) Murder as in the case of the much 'married' Smith.

I believe from experience that often both partners know that the 'marriage' is bigamous and go through it for any number of innocuous reasons of their own. Also that it is Bigamy on both sides.

In a country getting on for 60 million people it is easy – for many – to get lost, a change of name and departure to another part of the country, or abroad.

It is really quite easy to get 'married' again, here or abroad. Forgery and fraud are easy in this field, easier still in some places abroad.

Bigamy is usually not the crime it was. I say 'usually' because wilful desertion of a poor wife and young children can be serious. Otherwise it has merely added 'a technicality' to what is otherwise freely practised.

Finally I think that in the present day many know about or suspect 'bigamy' in others but do nothing about it. And yet again even in the case of an ordinary crime the Police do not come across it.

Conspiracy and Too Many Charges

I am firmly of the view that much of the trouble in our Criminal Law – time consumed, complexity, lack of understanding, strange decisions – is due to (1) the excessive tendency to allege conspiracy or a series of conspiracies and (2) multiplicity of charges.

It is almost traditional for the prosecution to do both. See for example all the reserve indictments in *R. v. Thompson and Bywaters*, 1922.

CONSPIRACY – When there are two or more accused (or even 'a person or people unknown') the first tendency appears to be to plead conspiracy or a number of conspiracies and cross-conspiracies, as well as the substantive charge or charges. I believe this adds nothing but complexity to the case. There are of course exceptions – but these should be occasional.

Conspiracy adds little if anything to a case, and can be taken into account by the judge when sentencing on the substantive charge.

The word 'Conspiracy' is easy to understand and is all too familiar to lawyers. But (a) it takes a long time to spell out to a jury, especially when there are two or more conspiracies (or

Cross-Conspiracies), (b) it takes a long time to prove and (c) it complicates and destructs the jury's thinking. We in the Law are all too apt to think that an unaccustomed jury think and react as we do. A jury likes things it can readily understand and not to be too weighed down by legal jargon. Even if counsel speaks of Conspiracy (much less two, three or four conspiracies) a judge can tell him otherwise when he has to Sum it all Up.

TOO MANY CHARGES – Criminal Law should not be turned into a game of chess – trying to cover all future moves, or into a form of pool, with permutations. It should be as clear, brief and simple as it can be.

Nearly every single act can add up to two or three offences. A thieves' outing at night could add up to twelve or more offences. But why charge all? Why not the main, more easily concentrated on, ones? I do not suggest just a single charge but as few as possible. In the particular case why not just have three – the stealing of the car and two (armed) robberies?

Why complicate by adding other offences about the car, attempted burglaries, unlawful possession of fire-arms etc. Counsel can readily separate four or five accused – but can a jury sort out readily which (if any) is Guilty and of which offence?

The policy should be 'The Less The Better' – not 'The More We have'.

A Peep into the Jury Room

There could not be three things clearer in English or Irish Law. One, the Court (Court of Trial or Court of Appeal, Criminal Division) will not listen to the jury or individual jurors after a verdict is given. Not for any purpose, but in particular not for any 'second thoughts' by a jury or jury person. Recantations are not permitted. Nor claims that: 'I didn't really mean guilty', 'I was so frightened', 'I was bullied'. 'How say you, members of the jury?' stops dead with the verdict. Two, to intimidate a juror during or after trial is contempt of court and punishable as such. Three, nobody has the right to ask a jury for their reasons. They need not, but can if they wish, disclose what went on in the jury room. Even the trial judge is not entitled to ask them for their reasons.

These three points were strongly underlined by the Court of Appeal, Criminal Division, in July, 1988.

One understands fully why English law will not tolerate jury or juror interventions after verdict given. Even if quickly given, for example, after hearing the antecedents or having heard Crown counsel ask for something which they had never known about. It may be his asking the judge for forfeiture of money found on the accused on arrest. Or for forfeiture of the accused's car.

Nor will the judge tolerate any jury representation as to the sentence he has Just passed. It could be a bold representation. 'We would never have convicted if we had known you would have given him that.' Or 'could not your Lordship be more lenient?' A judge has power to alter his sentence, within limits.

Now, understanding the Judicial approach to all this, I still feel niggles of worry about always excluding every post-verdict jury observation. Should not the court, first of all, allow *things* to be said? And, secondly, in very exceptional circumstances, be prepared to act on it? For example, if a juror claimed that he/she had been bullied into giving the guilty verdict he/she did. Duress, maybe even violence, within the jury room seems to me, with very great respect, so grave that *in exceptional circumstances the Court* (it would *probably* be the Court of Appeal by then) should have due inquiry made about such an allegation. Inquiry by, say, a judge alone and in camera. Then, if the Court of Appeal is not satisfied that the particular juror is lying, or wrong, quash the conviction or order a re-trial. A power to do this would almost certainly require parliamentary legislation. The power plainly does not *expressly* lie for the Court of Appeal, Criminal Division, to do this. Does it lie impliedly? I think arguably yes, but it would be safer to seek legislation.

What, readers, do you think? Do you share my feelings of discomfort at blank refusal to entertain post-verdict jury observations – or not? I recall, through my father, two Irish Bar stories for which he vouched. One, the County Cork jury who found the prisoner 'not very guilty'. The judge simply had to work that out with them and counsel. If I remember aright, he in fact interpreted

150

the verdict as one of 'Guilty' (Yes, 'Guilty') but containing a strong recommendation to mercy. The other story was of a County Kerry jury who returned to give their unanimous verdict of 'Not Guilty' with a new foreman, the former foreman sitting now in second place and bearing the signs of extensive exhaustion. These stories are not intended by me to be wholly facetious.

Contingency Fees

In these countries we have never had such a system; it has been frowned on as having many more disadvantages than advantages, and being open to serious abuses by unscrupulous lawyers. So much so that when I was a young barrister there was a 'shady' practice known as 'Ambulance Chasing' or 'Spec Litigation' which, if properly detected could get a solicitor struck off the rolls, or a barrister disbarred.

There are many forms of 'Contingency Fees'. The simplest, less open to abuse, is simply 'No Win – No Fee'. The really dangerous ones, as most of us lawyers think, are 'share in the award if you win' addition in the States; this has in places and at times got out of hand. This has further only been reviewable by the courts, in a very limited way, *e.g.* for people under mental disability and minors.

Is the 'Contingency Fees' idea a good one, or not? I, and many like me in the Law and outside it, think not, even in its most simple form of 'No Win – No Fee'.

The advantages are plain; a litigant (it does not apply in crime or family law matters), gets an actual case taken up professionally, without having to worry about fees.

Of the disadvantages there are four – (1) in 'share a proportion case', excessive demands and a later dissatisfied client; (2) a settlement against the client's interest to ensure success; (3) a tendency to cut down on evidence as far as possible; and (4) to avoid the best class of expert witnesses and to use the cheaper.

151

Treasure Trove

Bill Elverston came to see me in consultation – always one of life's more pleasant experiences, complete with the most unusual of cases.

'Ever heard of Treasure Trove, James?'

'Have you not heard of my standard work on the subject, Bill?'

'Oh of course, of course,' he said, 'it won the Booker Prize, didn't it?'

'I must say,' I said, 'I haven't had a larre practice in Treasure Trove but more than most.'

'Well I've got an old buffer who's got himself knee-deep in it at the moment. A chap called Lord Rockall – who owns about half of Shropshire and has been telling me for years that he can hardly keep the wolf from the castle door.

About a month ago this old fish was up on his hill field counting his sheep when he saw a group of them round a hillock and he caught a glimpse of something golden-looking. I must choose my words carefully – I wish he bloody well had – but by . . . by *searching* around he found this gold plate, three ancient gold necklaces, a half dozen elaborate bangles and five highly decorated rings.'

'Searching around you said?'

'That's my word. But he's a born old babbler and apparently he went round telling everybody that he searched round and dug them up with his hands. Never heard of the fact that they're the Queen's if they have to be dug up, only his if they're over- ground.

'Value?'

'Got them valued immediately. A million and a half plus.'

'Did he tell the Valuers how he got them?'

''Spect he did. By and large he's a truthful old bloke. Anyway he was about to get the stuff out when The Coroner's Officer called. He thought there was something up and swears that he simply said 'he'd found them'. He rang me immediately and I went down next day.'

'Did the Coroner's Officer see the site on the hill?'

'I expect he did, though our old fish says he didn't say a word about it. But given his frequent blabbering about it, it's as well known as Piccadilly Circus.'

'Anyway,' resumed Bill, 'the old coroner's whatnot took all the stuff away and there's to be an inquest next Friday. I hope you can manage it.'

'I'll ring Clem and he'll bring over the diary and see what we can manage.'

While Clem was on his way I asked Bill if he'd seen the hillock.

'Indeed I have. Looks as if a bull-dozer had been through it.'

'That's not showing your usual care-free optimism about your client's case.'

'Well frankly I have no optimism whatever about this particular client – he scuppers anything he lays hands on. A solicitor's dream.'

Clem came in with the diary. They greeted each other affectionately like the old friends they were. Anything that could be done for Mr Elverston would be done.

Clem managed and switched the engagements as only he could. 'I'll get Mr Moylan to do the two at Bow Street,' he said. 'Mr Dunn is free in the afternoon and can do the Registry case and I'll postpone the two Cons. That clears everything.' And to Bill he said, 'Who would you like as a junior?'

'That nice chap John Hamilton, if you've got him free.'

'Shall be done,' said – in one of his favourite phrases. When he'd gone I asked Bill did he know anything about the local Coroner.

'Pretty bloody I gather. Sort of monarch of all he surveys'.

'And how does our man get on with the locals, the people likely to make up a jury?'

'Surprisingly well, funnily enough.'

'I ought to see the mound myself before the inquest,' I said.

'If I drive you both down very early on Friday morning we could all have a look at it before Court.'

We fixed a time – 5 a.m.! And then went on to talk about possible witnesses.

'I think his head gardener and assistant would be a good idea,' said Bill. 'Highly thought of locally.'

'What could they say?'

'Well, unlike the old codger himself, they know what it's all about – and could speak about his not borrowing any spades or trowels or anything like that.'

'Any hope of any locals saying he found them on the soil?'

'Doubt it. But there may be a couple who didn't follow all his gossip.'

'What about his wife?'

'A good idea, James. Not that she can say anything, I expect. But she's a strong, impressive personality who does all sorts of good works.'

'And what about an expert of some sort?'

'What to do?'

'Just waffle about the subject. Perhaps define soil and earth and say how difficult they can be to differentiate.'

'I'll see what I can do.'

We believed that in this sort of inquest the Coroner had to have advance statements and we arranged that Bill's managing clerk, would go down next day, get the Statements and hand these into the Coroner's Officer. Meanwhile Bill would search for an expert.

Being Bill, he got him. Loads of degrees and learned letters. He got him down there to see the mound and to give a wonderfully vague but very learned sounding report.

When we got down there John Hamilton and I were horrified at the depredations.

We met the client; a most delightful old bugger, everything that Bill had said.

He hardly ever stopped talking, quite inconsequentially and often incomprehensively. All that he made clear – crystal clear – was that a million and a half or more would make life financially easier for him.

I took him aside and asked him, 'Are you quite sure that you found all these things on the surface and not buried down in the earth?'

'Oh yes, oh yes,' he said. 'Just covered over by leaves and nettles and things. Just what I've told everybody.'

'Very well,' I said. 'Now, when you give evidence, just stick to the first part. No more.'

We all arrived at the Coroner's Court about ten past ten. I was surprised to find that there was a young local barrister against me for the Crown instructed by a local solicitor. Both were extremely nice and friendly.

Both said to me, 'We've never done one of these cases, but you've obviously done many. What actually goes on?'

Ignoring the part about my experience I said, 'It's more or less like an ordinary inquest.'

'I've heard he's pretty rough stuff.'

'The most four-lettered man I've ever had the experience to appear before,' intervened his solicitor.

'A cross between an alligator and a crocodile,' added counsel.

'So one doesn't know what to expect?'

'Only that it's thoroughly objectionable and as a rule generally wrong,' said counsel.

'I've known his verdicts quashed by the High Court five times.' observed the solicitor.

At that moment the Coroner's Officer came over to us. 'I'm sorry to say Mr Smith has been taken ill. But I've been lucky to get the Deputy Coroner, Mr Grossman, and he's busy looking through the papers in his room. There will be a slight delay. I'll explain it to the witnesses and jurors in waiting.'

'Damn,' said my opponent with a smile, 'my clerk was going to ask for a further fee as risk money.'

At about 10 to 11 the Deputy Coroner came in, smiled at us and said 'Good morning, gentlemen.'

He was a small amiable, obviously good-humoured man. He said how sorry we all would be at Mr Smith's sudden illness. Nobody joined in.

'This,' he said, 'is a most unusual case. I've never actually tried one before, but unless counsel have any submissions to make, I propose to treat it as far as possible like any ordinary inquest.' We agreed.

The gold was set out on the table. The jury were sworn in and he explained to them very simply what the case was about. 'So it really is whether these items belong to the claimant or to the State in the person of the Queen?'

He then turned to me and said, 'In all Inquests and here I prefer counsel to call their witnesses in the ordinary way and to keep to normal Court procedure. Is that agreeable to you, Mr

Comyn and to you Mr Hoskins?'

We said a most approving 'Yes.'

He then said it was for me to begin and I told the jury that after the Coroner's preliminary speech there was no need for me to open the case. I called the client, his wife, the two gardeners and the expert.

Wholly unexpectedly (the Law is full of the unexpected) the client was brief and brilliant, even in cross-examination, which was excellent. When asked why the whole hillock had been considerably roughened up he simply said, 'That was after the discovery – to see if there was anything else there, which there wasn't.'

All his other witnesses were splendid. The Expert surpassed all expectations. He had four compelling reasons for supporting the Chairman's case – signs of surface 'parting' rather than digging, no sign of digging at the spot, the absence of any tool work and the ancients usually abandoned ornaments when in flight and over the years they've only been covered by 'surface covering'. He was challenged on his findings by the evidence of two archaeologists whom the Crown called. They said there was clear evidence of digging. They also called two men from different public houses ostensibly to say that they had heard the Claimant say that he had 'dug' for the gold. The first didn't come up to proof. The second agreed that he had also used a lot of other words to describe how he had found the objects. Moreover neither was able to explain why a lot of other people who had heard him had not come forward.

After speeches the Deputy Coroner summed up. It was a fair and very balanced Summing Up except that it appeared to us to come down at the end on the Crown's side.

The jury were out for less than a quarter of an hour and held that all the property belonged to the claimant.

The Coroner ordered it to be handed over to him – and as a mark of confidence he produced a small bag with tissue paper, in which he packed it.

When we came out of Court Bill said to me, 'Better bring out another edition of Treasure Trove as soon as you can – adding a new Chapter on this case.'

Judge Jeffreys — Jeffreys of the Bloody Assize

This tyrant of a judge is the wickedest these islands have ever known. Savage in his cruelty, brutal in his penalties, a vicious loud-mouthed bully in Court, a man who boorishly threatened recalcitrant witnesses (carrying out the threats), a drunkard. He had every fault which a judge should not have. He was born near Wrexham and called to the Bar in 1668. Amongst his earliest cases were the judicial hanging of well-known politicians and the trial of Titus Oates and Richard Baxter. Oates was pilloried, flogged and imprisoned for life, but the Revolution of 1688 set him free. Baxter was fined 500 marks and was held in prison until it was paid (which was eighteen months).

A rabid Jacobite he was sent on the Western Circuit – with other judges – to punish those involved with the unsuccessful Monmouth Rebellion. He was then Lord Chief Justice and a peer. Beginning at Winchester they visited six towns, including Dorchester. A total of 1,331 pleaded Guilty on various convictions. A total of sixty five people were hanged after the trials; some put the number at over three hundred. Over eight hundred prisoners were sentenced to transportation. Many others were subjected to brutal floggings. Jeffreys set the tone but it is to be remembered that there were other judges. Jeffreys is chiefly remembered on that Assize for the diabolical pleasure he took in his task and for his fury and invective from the bench.

Perhaps the worst of his trials was that of the widow, Lady Alice Lisle, in August 1685 in Winchester, when he found it hard to get her guilty of harbouring a rebel. After much haranging and bullying, the jury at first disagreed but were then forced to agreement, and he sentenced the accused to be burnt alive.

On his return he was promoted to Lord Chancellor. On James' flight he tried to follow but was caught at Wapping disguised as a seaman, drinking (as frequently) in a public house. He was taken to the Tower of London, already a dying man by reason of his excesses and died there in custody in April 1689, only in his forty-first year.

St Peter and Me

It was pouring from the Heavens as I stood outside The Golden Gates. Inside there was wonderful Sun.

I rang the Gold Bell. There was no answer. The man in the little silver Sentry Box was away. So I thumped the Diamond Knocker and almost immediately a doddering old man came hobbling down the path.

'Stop all that ringing and knocking,' he said. 'I'm nearly 2,000 and I can't walk very well.'

I recognised him as St Peter from the statues. 'I'm drenched,' I said, 'please let me in.'

'It's Thursday, our wash-day,' he said. 'A heavy wash today – a lot of draining.

'Please let me in, Your Holiness.'

'Can't,' he said, 'until I find out all about you. Who are you, anyway?'

'I'm Ronnie Ross from Rosslare.'

'That's funny,' he said. 'I don't think we've had anyone from Rosslare lately. You aren't codding me, are you – you don't mean Fishguard?'

'I'm not a Welsh-man,' I said haughtily. 'I'm Ronnie Ross, a farmer (adding) a small farmer.'

'I'll have to look you up in the Irish Book. You stay there,' and he toddled towards the Sentry Box.

I was drenched and tired, and I sat on the Rock of Ages until he came back.

'I can't let you in,' he said, 'there's too much against you.'

'But what have I done, Your Eminence?'

'I'll just give you three examples. Do you remember selling six firkins of butter at the Listowel Market, three of them with hefty stones?'

'They belonged to a cousin of mine.'

'That's the second thing – it's what you told the District Judge but he didn't believe you and you were convicted.'

'It was wrong. Anyway you know a bit about lying yourself,' I said naughtily.

Peter ignored that one. 'What about the cow you sold for the

Widow Callaghan? How much did you get for her?'

'£625, I think.'

'And paid the widow £600?'

'There were expenses.'

'Oh no there weren't. You sold her to a man in the next parish, who collected her free.'

'I think the widow woman gave me something for my trouble.'

'£25!'

'I perhaps didn't get as much as £625.

'Anyway I've been through the Seven Deadlies and you're in all of them.'

'All seven! Surely not Sloth?'

'Four instances of it – and Sacrilege as well.'

'Sacrilege?'

'Yes. When you were taking up the collection two years ago you pocketed two quid and put it on a horse, called Forbidden Fruit, who was beaten.'

'It was only by a short head, Apostle.'

'There's one other matter,' he said gravely. 'Another case of Sacrilege really. When you were living in Kerry did you by any chance destroy a Confessional at the local Church?'

'Five,' I said.

'Five – Heaven help us.'

'They were riddled with dry rot.'

'What had they got to do with you?'

'I was a building contractor in those days and very eager to do what was necessary to the Church.'

'How did the P.P. take it?'

'Pretty badly. He had to hear Confession in the open air for nine months.'

'You've got a right of Appeal against my decision to the Heavenly Court. Let me see now who are sitting for the Michael-mas Term. Ah yes – St Paul, St Joseph and St Patrick. He's Irish, we'll have to substitute St Andrew.'

'Can't I get in meantime – pending trial?'

'No. They sit outside at The Stone of Destiny – on a fine day.'

'Is there nothing at all to be said for me, Apostle? Not even that I got twelve caps for Ireland at Soccer and captained them three times.'

'I never knew that.' said Peter. 'Come in out of the cold at once. You're just the man to coach our team, for our annual match against Purgatory in eight weeks time.'

Financial Report

I was the natural choice last year to be Chairman of the Trustees of the Ushers' and Shorthand Writers' Extra Benefits Fund. After all I was for many years in charge of the Retired Wrexham Terriers' Dog Fund, the Disabled Horses' Trust and The Ageing Aberdeen Angus Cow Foundation. A pretty good record you'll say and you'd be right. This is the time for my first Annual Report and weighing it all up and looking to the future (as one must) I think everything is shaping well.

I have not met my Co-Trustees but we speak on the telephone.

I had if you remember £250,000 plus £5,000 (being my annual remuneration for an estimated five years).

We have £5,000 nestling in a Building Society (The Irish Temporary) gathering in $4\frac{3}{4}$% per day.

I invested £20,000 in Guinness (in what is known as a self-consuming investment) and they have gone up,

£20,000 each went into Irish and English premium bonds – recoverable at any time at par.

£5,000 was invested in Scratch Card Tickets. Unfortunately they only produced £3,500, mostly in twos.

£5,000 Irish Lotto and English Lotto were disappointing at a £10 return.

My Standing Order with the Pools is still standing but so far no returns.

£30,000 on the horses has realised £40,000, which is extremely good.

I invested £50,000 in Lloyds of London – Motor, Aircraft and Shipping Syndicate. Litigation is pending.

£30,000 went into Reuters. Where else can you get the news? Rising sharply.

£5,000 went into one of my personal favourites The Confetti and Cucumber group. Static at present.

£5,000 went into another of my old favourites, The Malaysia Aisle Rubber Company. They have branched out into a new line of business under the name of Carnations (Ireland) Ltd based on an island off Waterford.

So there it is. Coverage over a wide range (diversifying one's assets as it is called). I will keep my eyes open. I am at present thinking of concrete, rope and tape, as per one of my stockbroker's tips.

The Stockbroker's Letter

We'd surely stick if we were you
To what you hold in Scottish Glue,
For recently there's been a hum
That they will merge with Ghana Gum,
Who then in turn we think have hopes
Of tie-ups with United Ropes.
And if in fact these firms combine
They'll surely threaten Threaded Twine,
Who'll find themselves so awkward placed
They'll have to bid for Standard Paste,
Who as you know have got control
Of most (well, virtually the whole)
Of Plaster and Adhesive Tape,
The leading binders in The Cape.
So certainly the thing to do
Is not to part with Scottish Glue,
Especially since they've replied
That all the rumours are denied.

Counsel and solicitors acting bona fide in a case are the only persons recognisably prohibited (barred) from giving evidence about anything to do with the case. To have it otherwise would be to tamper with the very foundation of Justice.

Despite the Hippocratic Oath doctors are compellable to give evidence against a patient, criminally and civilly, however incriminating to the patients.

But what of confessors of all Religions? Catholicism is the best known ('the seal of the confessional') but there are many others, including a large number in the Church of England.

It is generally assumed now that – if pushed to its extremity (which it very rarely is) – a priest has no more privilege than a doctor. And if he refuses to give evidence he is guilty of contempt of Court.

I would dispute that the point is anything like as clear as stated. Shortly because (1) there seems to me nothing to show that the pre-Reformation legislation and practice have been revoked in this regard. (2) There are only a very few cases on the point in issue, and the express conflicting views, and (3) there is only one case I can find in this century bearing on the point – *Pais v. Pais*, 1971 PI 19 (Bake J as he then was).

There is no post-Reformation statute abolishing the right to confessions in secret – though it could be argued that the burden of anti-Catholic legislation implies it. But what of other Religions, like part of the Church of England, who have always regarded Confession as an unbreakable Sacrament? Then again what of the Emancipation of Catholics in 1830? The few decided cases of the 1800s were split both ways, and were decided 'on general principles'.

It was thought that *Pais v. Pais* in 1971 would decide the point, but it only held that a Catholic priest must give evidence of what has come to him on a conciliation meeting in a matrimonial dispute. It seems, however, to lean slightly towards Confessional Privilege.

Not unnaturally the Courts lean against an express view on the subject. In the cases where it seems to arise the Courts discourage it or find some way round, as happened in *Pais*.

In many other countries religious confessions are privileged by law.